Pure Vegan

Pure Vegan

70 Recipes *for* Beautiful Meals *and* Clean Living

by **Joseph Shuldiner**

photographs by **Emily Brooke Sandor** *and* **Joseph Shuldiner**

CHRONICLE BOOKS

SAN FRANCISCO

Text copyright © 2012 by Joseph Shuldiner.
Photographs copyright © 2012 by Emily Brooke Sandor and
Joseph Shuldiner.

Library of Congress Cataloging-in-Publication Data available.
ISBN 978-0-8118-7863-0

Manufactured in China

Designed by Joseph Shuldiner
Typesetting by Helen Lee
Prop styling by Dani Fisher
Food styling by Basil Friedman

The photographers wish to thank the following compa-
nies for their assistance in the production of this book:
Melissa's Produce, Earth Balance, Chado Tea Room,
GreenBar Collective, TableArt, Diamond Foam & Fabric,
and Cisco Home.

10 9 8 7 6 5 4 3 2 1

Chronicle Books LLC
680 Second Street
San Francisco, California 94107
www.chroniclebooks.com

Contents

Acknowledgments

Not a single page of this book would have been possible without the help, guidance, and support of so many people, and every page bears their imprint. The most significant imprint belongs to my partner and muse, Bruce Schwartz, and it permeates every aspect of this book, which he believed in even before I did. His abundant love and encouragement helped me to enjoy the successes and get me through the mishaps and bad ideas that got tossed out. His keen intuition and judgment became my litmus test whenever I needed a personal arbitrator of style, tone, or simply a kitsch-alert. I would also be remiss if I didn't mention the never-ending sink of dishes he constantly cleaned; only teasing that he wanted me to give him honorable mention for it.

Many events led me to writing this cookbook and one of the most influential was having met Susan Campoy. Sue was the owner of Julienne, the famed restaurant in San Marino, a 'burb of Los Angeles. We worked together closely for two years to produce her *Cooking with Julienne* book. Sue showed me how to be fearless and not stop at anything to get things just right.

Early on, when this book was just an unpolished idea, Kirsten Muenster and Joseph Ternes heaped on the encouragement and excitement I needed to propose this to Chronicle, and that is the best kind of support one could receive from friends.

While on the subject of Chronicle Books, you wouldn't be reading this if editorial director Bill LeBlond hadn't believed in me and guided this project to fruition. From there, my patient editor Sarah Billingsley cheerfully sifted my prose. Our easy back and forth was one of the great pleasures of writing this book.

I also owe a big thank you to my creative crew, lovingly referred to as "Team Vegan." First, Emily Sandor, who originally introduced me to Sue Campoy and who also inspired me to begin photographing food myself. She has been a great teacher and photo partner. The rest of my styling team was equally fantastic: Basil Friedman (food) and Dani Fisher (props) are the food equivalent of a celebrity's posse. They made all the dishes camera-ready for their close-ups and were a joy to work with. Assisting all our efforts were David Kiang, photo and digital technician; John Galanga, food styling; and Bella Foster, prop styling.

Early on when I was envisioning the recipes, I turned to Christine Moore, owner of Little Flower Candy Co. and her pastry chef Harriet Han Hayes for guidance with vegan baking. They graciously welcomed me into the café's kitchen to help me "veganize" a few of my ideas. The Pistachio Olive Oil Cake and Chocolate-Tahini Timbales were products of our late nights together. I consider Little Flower my satellite office and have held countless business meetings there when my kitchen was too full of dishes. (And thank you Christine, Harriet, and Robert for your 80-proof coffee!)

Creative vegan breakfast recipes are challenging in my opinion, but with the help of Chef Nick Coe's Kutya recipe, my mornings are much more exciting. When I heard that this Eastern European dish was being served at his Black Cat Bakery in Los Angeles, I asked Nick for the recipe, which he graciously shared.

Once the recipes were written, I depended on the feedback from an amazing group of home recipe testers. These home cooks were an amalgamation of friends, friends of friends, and a few Facebook acquaintances. Thank you James Aarons, Bob Brady and Kent Kirkpatrick, Cynthia Campoy-Brophy, Jennie Cook, Reed Davis, Merion Estes, Ashley Gish, Megan Hobza and the Veganistas collective, Courtney Hopkins, Gary Jackemuk, Karen Klemens, Erik Knudsen and Kelly Coyne, Tawnia Litwin, Stephen Rudicel and Gloria Putnam, Anne Schick, Heidi Spiegal, Nancy Sutor, Judith Teitelman and Aaron Paley, and Michele Zack. Many of the testers reside in different cities and our relationships were strictly via email and photos. My high school friend Heidi even tested recipes from Thionville, France, regaling me with stories of how she had to hunt down many of the ingredients. My best buddies Bob and Kent went as far as to shoot a video of their dinner party in New Mexico comprised exclusively of *Pure Vegan* recipes they were testing (show offs . . .). Many of the testers were vegans, and many were not. Regardless, the most frequent response from their experience was "I served this to guests and they had no idea it was vegan." That was the best feedback I could have heard.

Ingredient sourcing was one of the important components in creating the recipes and I want to thank a few of the distributors and producers for supplying ingredients during the many days of recipe development and photo shoots: Melissa's Produce, Earth Balance, Chado Teas, and GreenBar Collective.

Many of the photographs in this book would not have been possible without the warm generosity of Gloria Putnam and Stephen Rudicel for allowing us into their home, and historical monument, the Zane Grey Estate; Greta Dunlap, the South Pasadena Farmers' Market manager for letting us run rampant through the market aiming our lens anywhere we wanted; the Vartan family and their spice-filled Middle Eastern emporium, Vartans Family Groceries; and also the fecundity of rare and hard to find mushrooms on display at Dirk Herman's LA FungHi weekly market booth. (Mushrooms are the vegan's caviar!)

I also want to thank Blake Little for my author's portrait, Leslie Aiken for her emergency manuscript doctoring, and all of you who have been following the progress of *Pure Vegan* as it was being created.

My hope is that this is only the beginning and that everyone who helped with this book will come along for the next adventure. Please accept my heartfelt gratitude, one and all.

Introduction

Are you relaxed and sitting down? If not, turn to the recipe for Vegan Mary (page 36) and prepare yourself a batch. When you get back, we should have a little chat.

First, let me tell you what this book is *not*. *Pure Vegan* is not about politics or any kind of spiritual doctrine. My intentions in writing this book are not to debate the virtues of one belief system over another, nor to promote the health benefits of eating a plant-based diet. Aside from having little interest in these debates, I'm not qualified to take up a pair of boxing gloves in their defense.

Making my own day-to-day choices about what to eat and what not to eat is complicated enough without trying to tell you what *you* should and shouldn't eat. And that, my friend, is what this book *is* about: making choices that feel natural and right to you; to sow a few seeds in the back of your mind and help you cultivate your own plant-based culinary repertoire. No matter what dietary philosophy you follow, my hope is that reading and cooking from this compendium of recipes will inspire you to look at how you eat in a new way, sharpen your sense of relationship to the ingredients you encounter, and, above all, always demand more from the food you eat—more variety, more flavor, more intensity.

OPEN ALL NIGHT

In organizing the recipes in this book, I knew from the start that dividing dishes into the usual categories—appetizers, soups, salads, main courses, and so on—would bore me to death. I don't know about you, but I eat constantly, from morning to night. In fact, I've been ridiculed more than once for discussing tomorrow's breakfast as I prepare for bed.

That got me thinking about my preoccupation with eating and about what an important role food plays throughout my entire day, and this led me to organize the chapters by time of day rather than by type of dish. I made sure to include some late-night (and *very* late-night) recipes for you night owls out there who still crave a little something in the wee hours.

All too often, eating a plant-based diet can seem synonymous with self-deprivation and get in the way of late-night snacking desires. In *Pure Vegan*, I've attempted to liberate those desires with plenty of delicious options for impulsive, decadent dining at unusual hours—and perhaps unusual circumstances. That said, some of the recipes require a bit of forethought, so I suggest you plan ahead and prepare in advance as needed.

PURE VERSUS PURITANICAL

Instead of focusing on the foods eschewed in vegan cookery, my guiding principle has been to highlight and celebrate ingredients that are inherently vegan. Also, you'll notice that some of the recipes call for refined products (such as white flour), processed ingredients (like soy margarine), and, as you observed if you turned to the Vegan Mary earlier, alcohol.

I'm not at all shy about being a hedonist, which explains all the dessert and cocktail recipes, as well as the inclusion of a few ingredients that may border on the indulgent. After all, the title of this book is *Pure Vegan*, not *Puritanical Vegan*. It is my personal philosophy that certain guilty pleasures, like sweets and bad TV, keep us evolving when we indulge in them in moderation. (Besides, vodka is vegan.) If some of these ingredients offend your sensibilities, you can easily modify the recipes. Substituting whole-wheat flour for white flour is a no-brainer, though you should expect baked goods to be heavier and denser. Likewise, you can substitute a bland vegetable oil, such as canola for vegan shortening, but you will sacrifice some flakiness in the final texture. And when it comes to cocktails, you can easily "virginize" some of the recipes by simply omitting the alcohol.

EXOTIC INGREDIENTS

Some of the recipes and ingredients I've presented here may be new to you, but I'm confident you'll be curious enough to take them for a test-drive. Now that the Internet is everyone's permanent houseguest, hunting and foraging for most of the unusual items I call for is as easy as looking at the Web sites in the Resources section (page 216) and clicking "Add to Cart."

I grew up and continue to live in Los Angeles, a city where many ethnic groups have settled, sometimes in numbers so great that they approach the total population of their native countries. Living here has undoubtedly shaped my eating habits and given me a curiosity about exotic ingredients. I'm drawn to cuisines that embrace vegetables and feature dishes augmented by deep spice blends that elevate their flavor and complexity. Asian, Indian, and Middle Eastern cuisines in particular hold a special place in my culinary repertoire due not only to their reverent appreciation of ingredients but also to my adventurous culinary upbringing.

For those of you without easy access to some of these ethnic communities and their markets, the Resources section includes online grocers that stock everything you'll need. You can also substitute more common ingredients for many of the more unusual edibles I call for, but I suggest that you try any given recipe with the specified ingredients the first time. If nothing else, deciding on the right ingredients to substitute will be easier if you do.

MAKING THE CUT

While we're on the subject of following recipes, you'll find that sometimes the instructions are quite precise. For instance, you'll notice that I'm often specific about how thick or thin vegetables and fruits should be cut. This isn't just about how things look on the plate; it also has an impact on how they cook. If ingredients are all cut the same size, they'll cook evenly. Furthermore, the cut of an ingredient changes the way it is coated by a sauce or dressing; for example, the thinner the slice, the more surface there is to be coated with flavor.

I regret learning knife skills late in life. I highly encourage you to learn this art by renting a video or taking a workshop at your local kitchen-supply shop. It will add another dimension to your relationship with your ingredients. I also encourage you to make an investment in good-quality kitchen equipment if you haven't already. I'm not saying that you need every gadget in the world. In fact, most of the recipes in this book don't require specialized tools. But as my father-in-law liked to say, "It's important to use the right tool for the right job." See The Well-Equipped Vegan Kitchen (page 27) for a list of useful kitchen tools and cookware.

Ingredient Sourcing

In addition to steering our palates toward a plant-based diet, I feel strongly that we have a duty to pay close attention to the integrity of the ingredients involved. The origins of the foods we eat carries as much weight as what we eat. While you might think of this as something simply virtuous—for example, choosing local foods to lower your carbon footprint—I've found that digging more deeply into the true sources of ingredients can be one of the greatest pleasures there is.

A plant-based diet is simply that: eating plants. Given that they sustain you, why not build a committed, loving relationship with them? As any relationship counselor will tell you, therein lies the crux. Show the plants you eat some respect. Get to know everything about them: ask them where they're from, what their childhood was like, and who their friends are.

No one can deny that there's a huge difference between eating a zucchini that's just been pulled off its vine and eating one that was harvested weeks ago, trucked to one distribution center after another on its way to a chain "übermarket," then wrapped in plastic and sold on a plastic tray for your convenience. One tastes like a zucchini, full of sun and earth, the other tastes only slightly better than the plastic tray. Given the choice, it's obvious that we'd all prefer the real zucchini, but convenience can be a seductive trickster.

Growing your own vegetables, purchasing them directly from local farms or farmers' market, or otherwise creating a more direct connection to your food may seem like an overwhelming proposition. But I'm here to tell you it's not such a big deal. In fact, I have a food-sourcing pyramid guide that will address any anxiety you might feel when you think about having to make more conscious choices about ingredient procurement.

At the bottom of the pyramid is a foundation of organic foods. There is no reason why most of the ingredients you use cannot be organic. In the past, perhaps you could have complained about organic food being too expensive or hard to find, but that's history. As recently as 2000, I was on a plane and received the "veggie plate" I'd requested. My seatmate turned to me and asked if I was a health nut. We've come a long way since then. Today, organic is no longer just for nutcases; it's a multibillion-dollar commercial industry.

The bottom of the pyramid includes those übermarkets I chastised earlier, where most people buy their food—and where convenience so often trumps quality. In the past, it may have had a small, pathetic organic produce section near the employee's entrance. Though paltry, it was a start. If this describes your market today (or if your market has no organic products), I suggest you shop somewhere else or initiate a dialogue with your grocer, because the more we demand organic food, the more inexpensive and readily available it will become.

And then there's the Internet, where you can find anything your heart desires in seconds or less. There is nothing quite like the immediate gratification of cyberforaging (though of course you will have to wait for your goods to be shipped to you). One could quibble about the carbon footprint of purchasing items online that need to be shipped, but also consider the growing number of online businesses trying to make a difference by selling regional products produced using ethically and environmentally sound methods. Not all of us live in metropolitan communities, where there is easy access to healthful or unusual ingredients, but that's no longer a good excuse.

From that foundation, let's take a journey toward increasingly healthier and more meaningful food. Stepping up the pyramid, we arrive at farmers' markets. If you're imagining those "quaint" little shacks with hand-painted signs that you've seen on road trips, think again. Today's farmers' markets are a practical source for a wide variety of fresh, local foods. Almost every city has one, if not more than one, and many smaller towns have farmers' markets as well.

The idea behind these markets is simple: farmers, and small farmers in particular, can sell directly to customers at full retail price, without middlemen or übermarkets taking a percentage. What's more, farmers' markets give you a chance to speak directly to the person who grew the food, not just a produce clerk who stacks the apples. Ask the farmer questions about what they grow, and use what you learn to guide your choices. When was that zucchini harvested? What is its true growing season? Is it organic? And if it isn't organic, ask why. I guarantee you will begin a new relationship with your ingredients by getting to know the people who grow them.

Now we're going to climb a little farther up the pyramid. But as you've gotten used to asking some questions about your zucchini, maybe you find yourself interested in seeing its birthplace and touching the earth it grew in—maybe even picking it yourself. That's often exactly what you can do if you purchase a share in a community-supported agriculture (CSA) enterprise. At the next level of the pyramid, CSAs enable a farm to receive most of its operating expenses up front from people in the same community or region. You purchase a share of what the farm will produce in the upcoming season, and in return you get a selection of fresh, in-season produce directly from the farm at regular intervals. It may be delivered or distributed at a central location, or you may pick up your share at the farm, finally giving you that chance to see where that zucchini grew.

There's yet one more level above buying your produce directly from the farm that grew it. The next step in increasing the pleasure of eating is to grow some of your food yourself—to become the farmer. I know it's been a long time since you sprouted that lima bean in first grade, but it will all come back to you. Besides, "back to the land" is back with a vengeance. Front lawns everywhere are being replaced with edible gardens.

Even if you aren't ready to make that leap, you can still do something on a small scale. Even just growing tomatoes in a pot on your balcony qualifies you as an urban farmer, and in the process you'll learn some important lessons about what it takes to grow something from scratch.

Wherever you fall on this pyramid, I hope you see it as a journey—and an exciting exploration. And any time you gather ingredients to prepare a recipe in this book, I hope you'll consider making that exploration part of your eating enjoyment. You'll find that making well-informed choices adds new dimensions and depth to the pleasures of cooking and eating.

The Vegan Pantry

Whether you're stocking your vegan pantry from scratch or simply want to supplement your existing larder, here's a quick-start guide. It's not complete by any means, but I've attempted to cover the basics. I've also included information about some of the more unusual ingredients and what to look for when you purchase them.

ALCOHOL

My hedonist nature always steers me to the best-quality alcohol. Many large commercial producers make excellent libations, but with the rise of local, small-batch producers, I recommend going artisanal. More and more regions across the United States are becoming known for their wines, and many wineries aren't shy about promoting the fact that their grapes are grown organically (or even using the beyond-organic methods known as biodynamic). Spoiler alert: As with cane sugar, during the filtering process animal products can find their way into some alcohol products, particularly wines. Barnivore.com is a good source for finding out which brands are vegan friendly.

CHOCOLATE

Everyone seems to have a favorite brand or type of chocolate, so it's only fair that I get to talk about my personal favorite: bittersweet.

It's dark and just this side of bitter, and I feel I can taste the chocolate more than the sugar. Whether you eat it as is or use it in desserts, chocolate really needs only two ingredients: cacao and sugar. The percentage of cacao is also up to you, but make sure it's at least 65% cacao. Do read the label to make sure it's vegan, because other ingredients and additives are often used. I recently discovered ChocoVivo, a small, artisanal company that makes 65%, 75%, 85%, and even 100% organic cacao baking chocolate on a stone grinder. I'm working my way up the cacao percentage ladder!

COCOA POWDER

Available either as Dutch-processed or natural, cocoa powder adds an intensity to recipes when combined with dark or bittersweet chocolate. Dutch-processed cocoa is darker and has a nice, palatable flavor. It is also used when a recipe calls for baking powder, due to its alkaline nature. Natural cocoa is more bitter then Dutch-processed. It's more acidic, and when combined with baking soda, it creates beautiful leavened baked goods. Most of the recipes in this book call for Dutch-processed cocoa powder for its smooth flavor, though it would be fine to substitute natural cocoa, since none of those recipes contain baking soda.

COOKING SPRAYS

I admit that it's easy to grease a pan with oil or shortening by hand, but certain things appeal to my lazy side, and cooking sprays are one of them. They're available in a variety of plain healthful oil sprays from commercial conglomerates such as Pillsbury, as well as natural foods gentle giants like Spectrum. The gateway product that turned me was baking oil spray with flour, which coats pans with oil and flour all at once. Basil Friedman, the food stylist who worked on this book, was my pusher. When I read the labels on these products, they didn't seem as scary as I had expected: just oil, lecithin, and flour. Feel free to use the plain oil sprays when a recipe calls for greasing a pan, and baking spray oil with flour for recipes that call for greasing and flouring a pan. I have never had anything stick since I started using them. End of discussion.

DRIED FRUIT

Dried fruit is a great staple to have on hand, especially during the months when certain fruits aren't available. Apricots, figs, and dates are all great when you're craving something sweet. Sometimes sulfur dioxide is added, solely for visual reasons. Look for pure, unsulfured products.

FATS AND OILS

CANOLA OIL

Made from rapeseed, the seed of a hybridized version of the field mustard plant (or, more specifically *Brassica rapa*), refined canola oil has a much higher smoke point than olive oil. In other words, you can heat it to a higher temperature (450°F) without damaging the oil or having a negative impact on its flavor (not to mention avoiding setting off your smoke alarm). Canola is also considered a neutral-flavored or more bland cooking oil, which is helpful when you don't want the cooking oil to impart its own flavor to a dish. For optimum nutrition, choose unrefined or cold-pressed varieties, in which the seeds are not heated before, during, or after processing. Just take into consideration these have a lower smoke point than refined.

OLIVE OIL

Anytime you cook with olive oil, I recommend that you use extra-virgin olive oil (organic whenever possible). *Extra-virgin* refers to the first, or "virgin," pressing of freshly harvested olives. It is widely available and not too spendy, so there's really no reason to use anything else. Always purchase olive oil in dark glass bottles since it's sensitive to light and can quickly become rancid. It's also sensitive to heat, so here's a tip: fill a small bottle with enough olive oil for a few days' use and store the large bottle in your refrigerator or a cool, dark place.

VEGAN SHORTENING

Like many people, I grew up eating margarine, and for years it seemed that the vegan versions were a good option, whether for baking or spreading on bread. But that thick, buttery consistency is the result of the industrial process known as hydrogenation, and one of its downsides is the creation of trans fats—

now widely believed to be extremely unhealthful. For a time, there were few options to take its place. Eventually the Mediterranean diet came along, and many folks were content to dip bread in olive oil, but vegan baking still suffered. Enter Earth Balance. Their product line includes buttery vegan spreads and sticks and vegan shortening, which comes in half-cup, foil-wrapped sticks with tablespoon increment marks, making it easy to use and measure. Throughout the book I refer to "vegan shortening"; whether you use the buttery-flavored sticks or the more neutral vegetable shortening is up to you.

HERBS AND SPICES

A well-stocked spice cabinet is your secret weapon as a chef. Learning how to masterfully season dishes is a lifelong project, but here are a few things to think about: In terms of herbs, use fresh whenever possible for peak flavor. When purchasing dried herbs and spices, try to find a store that goes through its stock rapidly. That way there's a better chance that what you're getting is fresher and hasn't been sitting on the shelf for a year. Speaking of which, some people suggest that you apply the same rule to spices as is recommended for clothing in the back of your closet: if it's been sitting around for more than a year, toss it. I'll leave your wardrobe up to you, but it's a good practice to purchase herbs and spices in small quantities and replenish often. Opt for whole over ground and invest in a mortar and pestle or spice mill to grind them just before use. A Microplane grater can also be useful for grating larger spices, like nutmeg and cinnamon.

LECITHIN

I use liquid lecithin, a thick, sticky substance typically derived from soybeans, to keep those nasty ice crystals from forming in gelatos, and as an emulsifier in other recipes, to help stabilize mixtures that would otherwise tend to separate. Here's a little tip: When measuring liquid lecithin, oil your measuring spoon first. Then the lecithin will slide right out. (This is also helpful with nut butters and other sticky ingredients.)

NONDAIRY MILK

Soymilk is the most common nondairy milk because it most closely mimics the properties of cows' milk. I always use unsweetened soymilk so I can control the amount of sweetness in a recipe, but you can also use regular (unflavored) soymilk, except in savory recipes. Every brand is different, so if you don't already have a favorite brand, I suggest that you experiment with a few and see which you prefer. Almond milk can be substituted in a pinch, but note that it does taste like almonds. Rice, barley, hemp, and other alternative milks are all worth a try.

NUTRITIONAL YEAST

As with cilantro, most people seem to either love or hate nutritional yeast. Having firmly identified this drab yellow ingredient as hippie foodstuff, I wouldn't touch it for years. Now I'm a convert and use it—in moderation—whenever I want to add a little cheeselike pungency to a dish. It's available in powdered or flake form. I used flakes in all the recipes, but you can substitute powdered, using half the amount.

NUTS

I'm sort of nut crazy, and as you'll see, I use them quite a bit. Be sure to purchase nuts from a source with a high turnover to ensure freshness. Nuts contain oils that are sensitive to light and heat, so once you get them home, store them in the refrigerator to keep them fresh.

PEPPER

"Freshly ground pepper" is a mouthful, but in terms of flavor there is no substitute for whole black peppercorns that have just been ground. When you know you're going to be doing a lot of cooking, grind a few days' worth in a spice mill or with a mortar and pestle and stash it near your stove along with the kosher salt.

PRODUCE

FRESH VERSUS NOT SO FRESH

You'll figure out sooner rather than later that I'm all about fresh ingredients. However, fresh is only a baseline, a starting point, and substituting when necessary won't be the end of the culinary world. If not specifically noted, canned or frozen produce is usually substituted measure for measure. Dried fruit needs to be soaked in liquid to rehydrate, but it will never really "reanimate" to its original state unless you live in a sci-fi movie.

HERBS

Fresh herbs almost always impart more flavor than dried, but they aren't always available. A good rule of thumb when substituting dried herbs for fresh is to use one-third the amount called for. That said, certain recipes, such as summer rolls and pesto, obviously can't be made with dried herbs. Depending on your circumstances and green thumb, consider growing a few pots of herbs yourself. Though I'm lucky enough to have a garden, I also have pots of herbs growing in my kitchen, which cuts down on those last-minute forays into the garden with a flashlight.

MUSHROOMS

Fresh mushrooms are always my first choice, and that's what I specify in all the recipes that call for mushrooms. Feel free to experiment with different varieties. If all else fails, you can always use the ubiquitous button mushroom, though after trying oyster, chanterelle, or shiitake mushrooms, they will seem bland and tasteless. In a pinch, you can substitute dried mushrooms. Soak them in hot water for thirty minutes. When you drain them, don't throw out the soaking liquid out; after straining, it can be used as stock.

SALT

When salt is listed by itself as an ingredient, I'm referring to kosher salt. Coarser and less refined salt than common table salt, it has a purer flavor. You can, however, substitute table salt, using half the amount.

SWEETENERS

AGAVE SYRUP

A number of the recipes call for agave syrup, sometimes called agave nectar. Agave nectar is produced from the same plant from which tequila is distilled. It comes in both light and dark versions. Feel free to use either one in the recipes that call for it. It is a bit sweeter that refined sugar, and I've compensated accordingly.

MAPLE SYRUP

Maple syrup is simply the sap from maple trees, boiled down to concentrate its flavor and sweetness. I mostly use it for its distinct flavor, rather than as a sugar substitute. It comes in two grades: Grade A, which is more refined, and Grade B, which is less refined. Personally, I like the earthiness of Grade B, but the two are interchangeable.

SUGAR

Where recipes call for just plain sugar, I'm referring to granulated white sugar, and that's what was used in testing those recipes. Whether granulated white sugar is vegan or not is the subject of ongoing debate. To remove color, impurities, and minerals, refined sugar made from sugarcane is filtered through activated carbon, which may or may not be made from animal bone char. None of the char remains in the final product, but if you are concerned about this processing method, you may want to look for the word "vegan" on the package. Turbinado sugar, dehydrated cane juice, and date sugar are all possible substitutes for granulated white sugar. Another possibility is to seek out granulated white sugar made from sugar beets, since processing sugar beets doesn't require that filtration step. Unfortunately, sugar made from beets typically isn't labeled as such.

TAHINI

Tahini is ground sesame seed butter, pure and simple. Always stir the jar well to incorporate the oil that rises to the top of the jar when it sits on a shelf for any period of time. As with all nut and seed products, it's best to store it in the refrigerator or a cool, dark place to prevent it from becoming rancid.

TAPIOCA STARCH

Made from the dried root of the cassava plant, tapioca starch can be used as a thickener in puddings and gelato, and also as a glue for sealing spring roll wrappers. Tapioca is also sold in pearl form, but for the recipes in this book, be sure to purchase the finely ground powder (sometimes labeled as tapioca flour), which will dissolve quickly and smoothly.

TEA

I love tea, and I'm not afraid to move beyond the teacup and cook with it. If I could give you just one drop of tea wisdom, it would be "no teabags—ever." Whole tea leaves have far more flavor and integrity, whereas teabags typically contain a lower grade of tea made up of the crumbled or powdered leftovers after high-quality whole leaves have been processed. Just open up a teabag and see for yourself. Loose or whole tea is available both packaged and by the ounce in teashops, coffee bars, and all over the Internet.

TOFU

Whatever thoughts or feelings about tofu you bring to the table, you can't deny its versatility. It is made in a multitude of textures and densities and is practically its own food group. It comes in vacuum packs and in water in sealed plastic tubs in the produce or refrigerated section of the market, as well as in shelf-stable aseptic packaging similar to juice boxes (typically Mori-Nu brand). Depending on where you live, you might even be lucky enough to obtain it freshly made. The recipes in this book call for just two varieties, soft silken and extra-firm. Soft silken is smooth and custard-soft. I use it in sauces and for binding ingredients when I want to add protein to a dish without an obvious tofu presence. Extra-firm tofu is a substantial and primary ingredient in a few recipes. It is such a chameleon that it takes on the personality and flavor of anything it comes in contact with. I use extra-firm tofu as an ingredient in fillings to provide body, texture, and heft. Store any extra uncooked tofu in the refrigerator in water for up to a week, changing the water daily.

VEGAN MAYONNAISE

Follow Your Heart makes the best vegan mayonnaise, hands down. It has a great consistency. It's called Vegenaise, and you'll find it in the refrigerated section of any well-stocked grocery store. A few of the recipes call for homemade aioli, which is basically mayonnaise laced with garlic. I heartily recommend making it from scratch, but if you're short on time, mixing a few pressed garlic cloves into some Vegenaise will do the trick.

VEGETABLE STOCK

A good, rich vegetable stock adds flavor complexity to many savory dishes. Whether in soups, risotto, or sauces, it provides a foundation for the other ingredients to build upon. Widely available in ready-to-use cans and aseptic cartons, it also comes in concentrated powdered or paste form. Check the label and make sure there are no preservatives or chemicals listed. That said, the best way to assure the quality of your stock is to make it yourself. If you'd like to do so, you'll find a recipe on page 98.

WATER

Unless you have your own well or natural spring, you probably get your water from a chlorinated municipal water supply. While chlorine protects us from a number of water-borne disease-producing organisms, it can also have a negative impact on yeast, so use good-quality filtered water when making Ginger Beer (page 63) or the Twenty-One-Hour Boule (page 47).

THE WELL-EQUIPPED
Vegan Kitchen

Like a well-stocked pantry, a kitchen with a well-stocked arsenal of tools and appliances can elevate the experience of preparing meals. While it would be nice to have the entire list of recommended items that follows at your disposal, it may not be possible or even necessary to have them all. However, some of the recipes do call for specialized tools, so before making any recipe, always read it through to make sure you have not only the ingredients but also the equipment you need. Consider investing in a few quality items up front, then gradually building up your collection. Besides the enjoyment you'll get from using them, you'll also have something to leave to your descendants!

ALL THINGS MECHANICAL

BLENDER

Without a doubt, a blender's number-one reason for existence is to make margaritas. After that, it's a natural for puréeing soups and sauces. It can also fill in for a food processor, but aren't you sick and tired of ruining all your wooden spoon handles from trying to unclog the blades? Another option to consider is an immersion blender. This handheld device can be inserted directly into a cooking vessel to quickly purée a soup, sauce, or salad dressing without having to transfer the ingredients to a food processor or blender. The cleanup time this saves is a big plus.

CITRUS JUICER

While you can just slice your citrus in half and squeeze by hand, once you exceed a few lemons in a row, you'll want a tool that reduces your risk of a repetitive stress injury. There are a variety of types to choose from, including electric juicers, old-school cast glass juicers, handheld reamers, and hinged, clamping presses.

FOOD PROCESSOR

As mentioned previously, a blender can sometimes fill in for a food processor, but this appliance should definitely be part of your kitchen. In my view, it's as essential as a stove or refrigerator. I use the 11-cup model of the Cuisinart Pro. It slices! It dices! And it's big enough to handle larger volumes of food. At the same time, it's a fairly modest implement without too many bells and whistles. In addition to the metal blade, which is the primary workhorse, it has a number of shredding and slicing disks that make those tasks a bit more enjoyable.

ICE-CREAM MAKER

Believe it or not, when I was very young, my mom had a wooden-tub ice-cream maker. It was all very Main Street: we added salt and ice and took turns cranking the handle. Today, there are a number of inexpensive electric models available that make frozen desserts in twenty minutes, no hand cranking (or sore arms) required. Cuisinart makes a simple one that involves a canister you keep in your freezer, ready for your next adventure in gelato making.

PASTA MACHINE

Although I do make homemade pasta, I haven't included it in this book. There is, however, a recipe for Parchment Flatbread Crackers (page 120), which benefits from a tool that can roll out superthin sheets of dough. Many stand mixers have a fancy pasta-making attachment, but I like my Marcato Atlas hand-crank model. Atlas pasta machines have been used by Italian home cooks for decades. They clamp onto the counter and, with less elbow grease than you'd need for an antique ice-cream maker, crank out beautiful, paper-thin sheets of dough.

SPICE MILL

Small and reasonably priced (and sometimes masquerading as coffee bean grinders), spice mills are great for grinding small batches of spices from whole pods or seeds. I guess you could use your spice mill for grinding coffee too, but be sure to wipe it out afterward so your chai doesn't taste like a cappuccino.

STAND MIXER

I'm not a compulsive baker, but I do like my desserts, so I consider a stand mixer a guilty pleasure. Because all the parts on a stand mixer are fixed in place, you're safe from hazards sometimes encountered with a hand mixer, such as flying bowls and beater blades. A stand mixer also leaves you free to do other things during mixing, such as adding ingredients or sipping the chef's prerogative glass of wine. Depending on the model you purchase, you can also use a dough hook attachment to make bread and a whisk attachment to make salad dressing. While neither is impossible to do with a handheld mixer, once you've experienced using a stand mixer, you'll find it hard to go back.

THINGS THAT CUT
KNIVES

I feel compelled to deliver a sermon on the importance of investing in good-quality knives. When cooking plant-based cuisine, you will only need two or possibly three knives, so don't skimp. You'll need an 8-inch chef's knife, which will become your workhorse. Look for one with a solid, hefty handle that feels good in your hand, because you'll be constantly chopping, dicing, and slicing with this knife. A 3-inch paring knife is your other must-have. Use it for peeling and getting into those small crevices inaccessible to a chef's knife. Finally, if you feel like treating yourself, add a serrated bread knife to your collection. It will cut through a loaf of bread without reducing it to a deflated balloon, and it will also slice through a tomato like nothing else. One final note: Keep your knives sharp. If you don't want to sharpen them yourself, send them out to a professional on a regular basis.

MANDOLINE

The mandoline is a specialized tool that slices vegetables thinly and evenly—and at warp speed. Just beware; its razor-sharp blade means you need to be careful to keep your fingers and knuckles out of the way. Most mandolines come with a safety handle to help you avoid accidents.

MICROPLANE GRATERS

How did we ever live without Microplane graters? Outshining a box grater, these amazing tools can grate chocolate, carrots, hard spices like whole cinnamon and nutmeg, and, most important, citrus zest and ginger. They come in a variety of sizes and shapes and with different sizes of holes, so start with the one you think you'll use most often, or splurge and get several.

VEGETABLE PEELER

If you don't have a vegetable peeler, put down this book and go buy one immediately. They're typically about the price of a pound of organic potatoes but will last a lifetime. You could use your new paring knife as a peeler, but you'll inevitably remove a lot of the vegetable along with the skin. Either a Y-peeler or a swivel peeler will do; just make sure your vegetable peeler is sturdy and has a comfortable handle.

THINGS THAT STIR
FLEXIBLE SPATULAS

I like to have at least three spatulas always at the ready. "Small, medium, and large" is the mantra here. Spatulas are indispensable for scraping every last bit of ingredients from a bowl, spreading things out nicely and neatly, or getting the last drop of mustard from the bottom of the jar. Choose good silicone spatulas that won't split or melt under high heat conditions.

SPOONS

If I have way too many juicer gadgets, my spoon collection qualifies me for my own segment on the TV show *Hoarders*. Most people bring home knickknacks or local delicacies from their foreign travels. I bring home wooden spoons. Long-handled, perforated, flat, angled, slotted, I use them all and feel they're as indispensable as a good knife.

WHISK

A whisk is perfect for incorporating air into batters, and also for clobbering clumps. Get one that's sturdy and won't need replacing in a month.

THINGS THAT MEASURE
KITCHEN TIMER

I have a digital kitchen timer, and I use an app on my phone as backup when I need to time more than one item. If, like me, you're easily distracted, a timer with a loud, obnoxious alarm is the best bet.

MEASURING SPOONS AND CUPS

You'll need a set of measuring spoons and a set of measuring cups, either plastic or metal.

SCALE

Having a real kitchen scale separates the men from the boys (not to mention the women from the girls). Though U.S. cookbooks often call for measuring by volume, this isn't as accurate as measuring by weight. Among other things, ingredients can vary in density; for example, mushrooms or cheese. In this book I occasionally call for ingredients by weight, so it might help to have a scale handy. And even if you don't often need it for the recipes in this book, it's simply a good piece of equipment to have on hand.

THERMOMETERS

You will need a thermometer for measuring the temperature of some of the liquids in the recipes. Kitchen thermometers come in two styles: instant-read and digital. Either one is fine. Just make sure it's easy to read and can measure up to 400°F if you plan on making the Tea-Poached Pears with Caramel Sauce (page 188) or Hazelnut Halvah (page 203) recipe. And while you're at it, I recommend that you pick up an oven thermometer. No matter how new or top-of-the-line your oven is, it could be off by as much as 25°F to 50°F.

THINGS THAT CONTAIN

BOWLS

You'll need at least a few mixing bowls. Depending on how elaborate my menu is, I may have as many as six bowls going at a time. For your average meal, however, the "small, medium, and large" mantra applies. Be sure to have some bowls that can take heat, such as Pyrex or metal.

COCKTAIL SHAKER

Instant panache! A jar with a lid will work just fine, but wouldn't you rather show off a little and impress your guests?

COLANDER

Not to be confused with a sieve (see following), a colander has larger holes and is meant for rinsing or draining large items such as pasta, vegetables, or beans. I suggest finding one as large as your kitchen can accommodate. There are few things as irritating as an overflowing colander.

FINE-MESH SIEVE

Not to be confused with a colander (see preceding), a fine-mesh sieve strainer is used to drain fine ingredients and strain liquids, as well as dust the top of desserts with cocoa and sugar. You can also use it to smooth out lumpy batter; just use the back of a large spoon to push the batter through the mesh.

PLASTIC SQUEEZE BOTTLES

Squeeze bottles are great for emulating the styling of pretentious restaurants, which can be a nice touch when cooking for company. Use them to apply sauces or salad dressings. You'll avoid drips and splatters, and if you're feeling creative, you can make pretty patterns on the plate.

THINGS THAT YOU COOK IN OR ON

BAKING SHEETS AND PANS

Invest in a heavy, professional-quality set of baking pans and sheets. You won't regret it. Start with a couple of 13-by-18-inch baking sheets that won't warp in the oven. Then add a 5-by-9-inch loaf pan and a 9-inch round cake pan. I also recommend a 9-inch springform pan with a removable bottom.

POTS AND PANS

You may have inherited your set of pots and pans from your parents, or maybe you never got rid of that old set you had in college. Whatever the case may be, if you're frustrated or unhappy with what you have, for goodness sake, go out and buy new cookware. There are a multitude of brands and materials to choose from. Copper-bottomed pans conduct heat most efficiently, though there's something about cast iron that feels earthy, and it also holds heat once it's warmed up. Do a little research, ask friends what they prefer, and read reviews. It's a personal thing, and I'm sure you'll know when you've discovered the set that feels right. Just be sure to have a variety of sizes of pots and pans on hand. You'll need small, medium, and large skillets or sauté pans for sautéing. You'll also need two or three saucepans with lids, as well as a large soup pot.

SILICONE BAKING MAT

Sort of a miracle material, silicone can withstand up to 500°F in the oven, and nothing seems to stick to it. A silicone baking mat lies right on the baking sheet, so you don't have to grease the pan or use parchment paper.

TART PANS

You'll need at least one tart pan if you plan on attempting any of the tart recipes in this book. Start with a classic round pan with fluted edges and a removable bottom. I usually specify a 9-inch tart pan, but once you get the hang of making tarts, you can experiment with making small, 4½-inch individual tartlets, such as the Savory Breakfast Tarts (page 44) instead of one large tart.

CHAPTER 1

Morning

Chai Tea

Served throughout India, chai is a warm, fragrant combination of tea, spices, and milk. This exotic beverage is a great way of exploring some spices that may seem unusual to you. I named this version after the West Bengal narrow-gauge steam train that, in the late 1800s, opened up the Darjeeling tea-growing region to travelers. As I sip this tea, I like to daydream that I'm sitting in a train station in the clouds, waiting for the DHR to refuel its steam engine before ascending to the tea fields.

──────────────────────────{ **SERVES 4** }──────────────────────────

1 **tablespoon fennel seeds**

1 **tablespoon cardamom pods**

6 **cloves**

6 **black peppercorns**

1 **cinnamon stick, broken into a few pieces**

One **2-inch piece fresh ginger, unpeeled, thinly sliced**

1 **bay leaf**

3½ **cups filtered water**

2 **tablespoons Darjeeling or other black tea leaves**

1 **cup plain soymilk**

Sugar

In a mortar, combine the fennel seeds, cardamom, cloves, peppercorns, and cinnamon stick and use the pestle to crush them just until they release their fragrance. Alternatively, put the spices on a cutting board and give them a few good pounds with the bottom of a heavy skillet. The spices should merely be cracked, so be sure to stop before they turn to powder.

In a medium saucepan, combine the crushed spices, ginger, and bay leaf. Pour in the water and bring to a boil over medium-high heat. Lower the heat and simmer, uncovered, for 10 minutes.

Remove from the heat, add the tea leaves, and let steep for 5 minutes. Strain immediately, discarding the tea leaves and spices. Stir in the soymilk and sweeten with sugar as desired. Return the tea mixture to the saucepan and bring back to a simmer, then remove from the heat immediately. Serve in warmed teacups or mugs.

Vegan Mary

Who says going vegan means never having any fun? As far as Bloody Marys go, those bothersome anchovies used to make traditional Worcestershire sauce are the only sticking point. I've taken care of that with a homemade, anchovy-free version I call Veganshire Sauce. This recipe for the classic cocktail calls for aquavit, a Norwegian liquor made from potatoes and flavored with caraway, but you could also substitute a high-quality vodka. Rise and shine!

··{ **SERVES 4** }··

16 ounces tomato juice

4 ounces aquavit

2½ ounces fresh lemon juice

1 teaspoon Veganshire Sauce (page 38)

1 teaspoon Tabasco sauce

1 teaspoon finely grated peeled fresh horseradish or prepared horseradish

Freshly ground pepper

Ice cubes

4 celery stalks for garnish

4 halved cherry tomatoes for garnish

4 lemon wedges for garnish

In a pitcher, combine the tomato juice, aquavit, lemon juice, Veganshire Sauce, Tabasco, horseradish, and pepper and stir until well mixed. (At this point, the mixture can be covered and refrigerated overnight.)

Fill four glasses with ice and divide the tomato juice mixture among them. Garnish each glass with a celery stalk, 2 cherry tomato halves, and a lemon wedge speared on a cocktail pick, then serve.

Veganshire Sauce

6 tablespoons water

6 tablespoons molasses

¼ cup soy sauce

2 tablespoons apple cider vinegar

1 small shallot, minced

¼ teaspoon minced garlic

¼ teaspoon minced peeled fresh ginger

1 teaspoon ground ginger

½ teaspoon sea salt

⅛ teaspoon cayenne pepper

⅛ teaspoon ground cloves

In a medium saucepan, combine all of the ingredients. Bring to a boil over medium-high heat, stirring occasionally. Continue to boil for 2 minutes, stirring constantly. Remove from the heat and let cool. Pour the mixture into a blender and blend until smooth. Strain if you'd like a smoother sauce. Store in an airtight container in the refrigerator; the sauce will keep for up to 3 months.

Breakfast Fries

These baked, thickly cut, and richly spiced potatoes are a nice change of pace from the more conventional home fries or hash browns. Of course, you can make these any time of day, but preparing them for breakfast feels special somehow.

{ **SERVES 4** }

2 **large russet potatoes**

¼ **cup extra-virgin olive oil**

2 **garlic cloves, minced**

2 **teaspoons smoked Spanish paprika**
   Salt

½ **teaspoon ground cumin**

¼ **teaspoon cayenne pepper**

¼ **teaspoon freshly ground pepper**

Preheat the oven to 400°F. Line a rimmed baking sheet with parchment paper.

Cut the potatoes in half lengthwise, then slice the halves lengthwise into ½-inch-thick wedges. Fill a large bowl with cold water and soak the potatoes for 1 minute to remove the starch. Drain and repeat two or three times, until the water runs clear. Drain again, then dry the potatoes with a clean kitchen towel.

In a large bowl, combine the olive oil, garlic, paprika, 1 teaspoon salt, cumin, cayenne, and pepper and stir until well mixed. Add the potatoes and toss until evenly coated. Arrange the potatoes in a single layer on the prepared baking sheet.

Bake for 30 minutes, then turn the fries over and bake for 30 minutes more, until crispy and browned. Season with more salt if desired and serve hot.

Multigrain Kutia
WITH ALMONDS, CHERRIES, AND CHOCOLATE

Sometimes I get tired of oatmeal. I still crave a warm bowl of cooked cereal in the morning, but I want one that's elevated, with unexpected flavor and texture. I found just that at the Black Cat Bakery in Los Angeles, where Chef Nick Coe offers up *kutia*, a Ukrainian porridge traditionally prepared with whole wheat berries, then garnished with fruits and nuts, and served during the Easter and Christmas holidays. Nick generously shared his recipe with me—a modern version that flirts with a combination of grains from three different regions: quinoa, a South American staple; farro, an ancient variety of wheat that hails from Italy (look for *farro perlato*, the semipearled type, which cooks faster); and kasha, or roasted buckwheat groats, a nod to the Slavic. This recipe makes enough for an extended Ukrainian family, but the cooked grains keep well in the refrigerator and are easily reheated, making for a quick breakfast throughout the week.

{ **SERVES 6 OR 7** }

ALMOND MILK

- 2 cups raw almonds (9 ounces)
- 5 cups water
- One 2- to 3-inch cinnamon stick, broken in half
- ¼ cup agave syrup or maple syrup

- ½ cup sliced or slivered almonds (2 ounces)
- 1 cup semipearled farro
- 1 cup kasha
- 1 cup quinoa
- 4½ cups water
- ½ teaspoon salt
- ½ cup dried cherries
- 2 ounces dark chocolate, coarsely chopped

TO MAKE THE ALMOND MILK: Put half of the almonds and water in a blender and add half of the cinnamon stick. Blend until creamy and smooth, about 2 minutes. Put a fine-mesh strainer over a bowl and pour the mixture through, pressing the solids with the back of a wooden spoon to extract as much of the almond milk as possible. Discard the solids. Blend and strain the remaining almonds, water, and cinnamon in the same way.

Stir in the agave syrup, then refrigerate for at least 1 hour and up to overnight to allow the flavors to develop.

Preheat the oven to 350°F.

Spread the almonds in an even layer on a rimmed baking sheet and bake for 10 to 15 minutes, until lightly toasted and fragrant.

Rinse the farro, kasha, and quinoa separately under cold running water until the water runs clear. In a small saucepan, bring 1½ cups of the water to a boil. Add the farro and ¼ teaspoon of the salt. Lower the heat, cover, and simmer until all of the water has been absorbed and the grains are tender but not mushy, 25 to 30 minutes. Remove from the heat and let stand for 5 to 10 minutes for a final steaming.

Meanwhile, in a medium saucepan, bring the remaining 3 cups of water to a boil. Add the kasha, quinoa, and remaining ¼ teaspoon salt. Lower the heat, cover, and simmer until all of the water has been absorbed and the grains are tender but not mushy, 15 to 20 minutes. Remove from the heat and let stand for 5 to 10 minutes for a final steaming.

In a large bowl, combine the farro, kasha, and quinoa and gently fluff with a fork. Portion about 1 cup of the grains into individual bowls. Pour ¾ cup almond milk over each helping of porridge and top with some of the toasted almonds, cherries, and chocolate before serving.

TIP: To prepare *kutia* in advance, spread the cooked grains in an even layer on one or more baking sheets and let cool completely. Transfer to an airtight container and refrigerate for up to 1 week. To reheat, put the grains in a saucepan and add ¼ cup of water per 3 cups of grain. Cover and cook over medium-low heat for 5 to 10 minutes to gently steam grains, then serve as directed.

Savory Breakfast Tarts

These tarts provide for those special needs we have in the morning—a hearty start to the day, as well as something a little decadent in the pastry department. I went for the earthiness of wild mushrooms and thyme in this version, but I encourage you to experiment with other fillings, such as a combination of leeks, squash, potatoes, and rosemary. Note that this recipe calls for eight individual tart pans with removable bottoms, so you'll need to have those on hand. You can also make one larger tart using a 9- or 10-inch tart pan.

··{ **SERVES 8** }··

CRUST

- 1½ cups all-purpose flour, plus more for dusting
- ½ cup hazelnuts (2 ounces), toasted and skinned (see Tip, page 203) and coarsely chopped
- 1 teaspoon sea salt
- ½ cup cold vegan shortening, diced
- ¼ cup ice water, or as needed

FILLING

- 6 tablespoons extra-virgin olive oil
- 2 leeks (white and pale green parts only), well cleaned and thinly sliced
- 1 pound mixed wild mushrooms (such as oyster, chanterelle, and stemmed shiitake), sliced
- 1 teaspoon sea salt
- 1 tablespoon chopped fresh thyme
- One 12.3-ounce container soft silken tofu, drained
- ½ cup unsweetened plain soymilk
- 3 tablespoons nutritional yeast flakes

CONTINUED

TO MAKE THE CRUST: In a food processor, combine the flour, hazelnuts, and salt and pulse until the nuts are finely ground. Add the shortening and pulse until the mixture resembles a coarse meal. Add the ice water 1 tablespoon at a time while continuing to pulse. Stop as soon as the dough comes together.

Transfer the dough to a work surface and divide it into eight equal pieces. Pat each piece into a disk. Wrap the disks individually in plastic wrap and refrigerate for at least 30 minutes and up to overnight.

Transfer the chilled dough to a lightly floured work surface and roll each disk into a 6-inch round; if the dough is too sticky, you can sandwich it between two sheets of parchment paper or plastic wrap for rolling. Transfer the rounds to eight 4½-inch tartlet pans with removable bottoms. Gently press the dough against the bottom and sides of the pans, then refrigerate the tart shells for 20 minutes.

Preheat the oven to 400°F.

Put the tartlet pans on a rimmed baking sheet and bake for about 15 minutes, until the crusts are pale golden. Remove from the oven and let cool on a rack.

MEANWHILE, MAKE THE FILLING: In a large, heavy skillet, heat 3 tablespoons of the olive oil over medium heat. Add the leeks and sauté until tender, about 4 minutes. Add the mushrooms. Sprinkle ½ teaspoon of the salt over the mushrooms, raise the heat to medium-high, and sauté until the mushrooms are tender, about 8 minutes. Add the thyme and sauté for 1 minute. Transfer the mushroom mixture to a bowl and set aside to cool.

Lower the oven temperature to 375°F. In a blender or food processor, combine the tofu, soymilk, nutritional yeast, remaining 3 tablespoons olive oil, and remaining ½ teaspoon salt and blend until smooth and creamy. Pour the tofu mixture into the mushrooms, stir until well combined, then spoon the mixture into the prepared crusts.

Bake for about 30 minutes, until the filling is set and beginning to brown on top. Let stand for 10 minutes, then remove the tarts from the pans and serve.

TWENTY-ONE-HOUR

Boule

Don't be alarmed by the twenty-one hours in the title. You'll only have to devote ten minutes of your precious time to this miraculous loaf of bread, which practically bakes itself. The rest of the time you'll be dreaming about that first, heavenly bite. Inspired by the no-knead bread recipe made famous by Jim Lahey, owner of Sullivan Street Bakery in New York, this boule gets its name from a traditional round French rustic loaf, with a shape resembling the ball (*boule* in French) used in the game *pétanque*. The only specialized piece of equipment you'll need is an ovenproof Dutch oven with a lid. Alternatively, you can bake the bread on a pizza stone and cover it with a deep ovenproof pot, or use any ingenious combination that will encase the boule and give it plenty of room to double in size when it rises during baking. The main thing to watch out for is pot and lid handles that aren't ovenproof.

························{ **MAKES ONE 2-POUND LOAF** }························

3¾ **cups bread flour, plus more for dusting**

¼ **cup vital wheat gluten**

¼ **teaspoon active dry yeast**

1½ **teaspoons salt**

1¾ **cups filtered, unchlorinated water**

In a large bowl, combine the flour, vital wheat gluten, yeast, and salt and stir until well mixed. Add the water and stir until well blended. The dough should be wet and fairly sticky. Cover the bowl with plastic wrap and let the dough rest in a warm spot (about 70°F) for 18 hours.

CONTINUED

After its 18-hour rise, the dough will have at least doubled in volume and will have small bubbles forming on the surface. Using a flour-dusted dough scraper or spatula, scrape the dough onto a clean, lightly floured work surface. Coat your hands with flour, then gently pat the dough with your palms to create a thick disk. With both hands, gently reach under the dough and lift and stretch the disk just a few inches to form an oblong shape. Set the dough back down and fold the short ends in, just like folding a letter. Rotate the disk 90 degrees and repeat the lifting, stretching, and folding.

Flour your hands again and shape the dough into a ball by tucking the outside edges underneath as you quickly rotate the ball through a few 90-degree turns in your hands. The ball should start to form a nice smooth surface on top. Don't fret over this step; each time you make this loaf you'll get more familiar with the bread and how to shape it.

Create a *banneton* (traditionally a wooden basket used to shape certain loaves prior to baking) by lining a basket or 9- to 10-inch-wide bowl with a lint-free tea towel. Generously coat the towel-lined bowl with flour, then put the ball of dough on the towel, seam-side down. Dust with more flour and cover with another tea towel, then let the dough rise for 2 hours, until it doesn't readily spring back when poked with a finger.

About 30 minutes before the end of the second rise, put a lidded 6- to 8-quart Dutch oven or heavy ovenproof pot in the oven and preheat to 475°F.

Once the oven has preheated for 30 minutes, carefully remove the pot from the oven. Remove the top tea towel from the dough and lift the dough by grabbing the tea towel liner at both ends. Slide one hand under the towel and flip the dough over into the pot, seam-side up, gently coaxing the towel away from the dough if it has stuck anywhere.

Cover the pot and bake for 30 minutes. Uncover and bake 15 to 30 minutes more, until the boule is browned and sounds hollow when tapped. Remove from the oven and immediately transfer to a rack to cool. Transfer to a cutting board, slice, and serve.

French Toast

WITH CARDAMOM PEAR COMPOTE

French toast, that childhood comfort food, gets a grown-up play date with a cardamom-scented pear compote. Be sure to use a good-quality maple syrup and homemade bread or at least a loaf of rustic country bread from a local bakery. The compote can be prepared the night before.

{ **SERVES 6 TO 8** }

COMPOTE

- 2 **pears, peeled and cored**
- ⅓ **cup maple syrup**
- **Grated zest of ½ lemon**
- 1 **tablespoon fresh lemon juice**
- ½ **teaspoon ground cardamom**

FRENCH TOAST

- 1 **cup all-purpose flour**
- 1 **teaspoon ground cinnamon**
- ½ **teaspoon salt**
- 1¼ **cups soymilk**
- 1 **tablespoon maple syrup, plus more for drizzling**
- 1 **teaspoon pure vanilla extract**
- 1 to 2 **tablespoons canola oil or soy margarine**
- 6 to 8 **slices rustic bread, preferably Twenty-One-Hour Boule (page 47)**
- **Powdered sugar for dusting**

TO MAKE THE COMPOTE: Cut the pears into ½-inch dice. Put them in a small saucepan over medium-high heat; add the maple syrup, lemon zest, lemon juice, and cardamom; and bring to a simmer. Lower the heat and simmer, stirring occasionally, until the mixture is thick and syrupy, 10 to 20 minutes. Remove from the heat and cover to keep warm. (If you make the compote in advance, reheat before serving.)

TO MAKE THE FRENCH TOAST: In a medium bowl, combine the flour, cinnamon, and salt and blend with a whisk. Add the soymilk, maple syrup, and vanilla and whisk just until smooth and free of lumps.

In a large skillet, heat 1 tablespoon of the canola oil over medium-high heat until a drop of water sizzles when added to the pan. Dip several slices of the bread (however many will fit in the skillet without touching) in the batter and fry until golden brown on the first side, 1 to 2 minutes. Turn and fry the second side until golden brown. Repeat with the remaining bread, adding more oil as necessary. Serve with the pear compote and a dusting of powdered sugar. Drizzle with additional maple syrup if desired.

Breakfast Strata

Preparing this layered, baked casserole may take a little time, but it's the perfect dish for a lazy weekend with guests. Encased in a flaky dough, this morning showstopper is as beautiful to look at as it is to eat. Each slice reveals the multi-colored strata, or layers of ingredients. You can assemble it a day ahead and just pop it in the oven the next morning. Just be aware that even once you put it in the oven, it won't be ready to serve for another two hours. No worries; that will leave you plenty of time to lounge around in your pajamas and mix up a batch of Vegan Marys (page 36).

{ SERVES 10 }

DOUGH

- 2 cups all-purpose flour, plus more for dusting
- 1 teaspoon salt
- ½ cup cold vegan shortening, diced
- ¼ cup ice water, or more as needed
- 1 teaspoon olive oil

SCRAMBLED TOFU

- 1 tablespoon extra-virgin olive oil
- 1 tablespoon minced garlic
- 2 teaspoons ground cumin
- 1 teaspoon smoked Spanish paprika
- ½ teaspoon turmeric
- ½ teaspoon salt
- ¼ cup nutritional yeast flakes
- 1 pound extra-firm tofu, drained, pressed (see Tip, page 166), and crumbled

CASHEW CREMA

- ¾ cup raw cashew pieces (4 ounces)
- 2 tablespoons fresh lemon juice
- 1 garlic clove
- 1 tablespoon extra-virgin olive oil
- 8 ounces extra-firm tofu, drained
- ½ teaspoon salt
- 1 or 2 grinds of pepper

FILLING

- 3 pounds red or green chard (3 to 5 bunches), or 1 pound spinach
- 3 tablespoons extra-virgin olive oil
- 12 ounces shiitake or cremini mushrooms, stemmed and sliced
- 1 cup fresh basil leaves
- One 8-ounce jar roasted red bell peppers, drained and patted very dry with paper towels
- 1 tablespoon unsweetened plain soymilk

CONTINUED

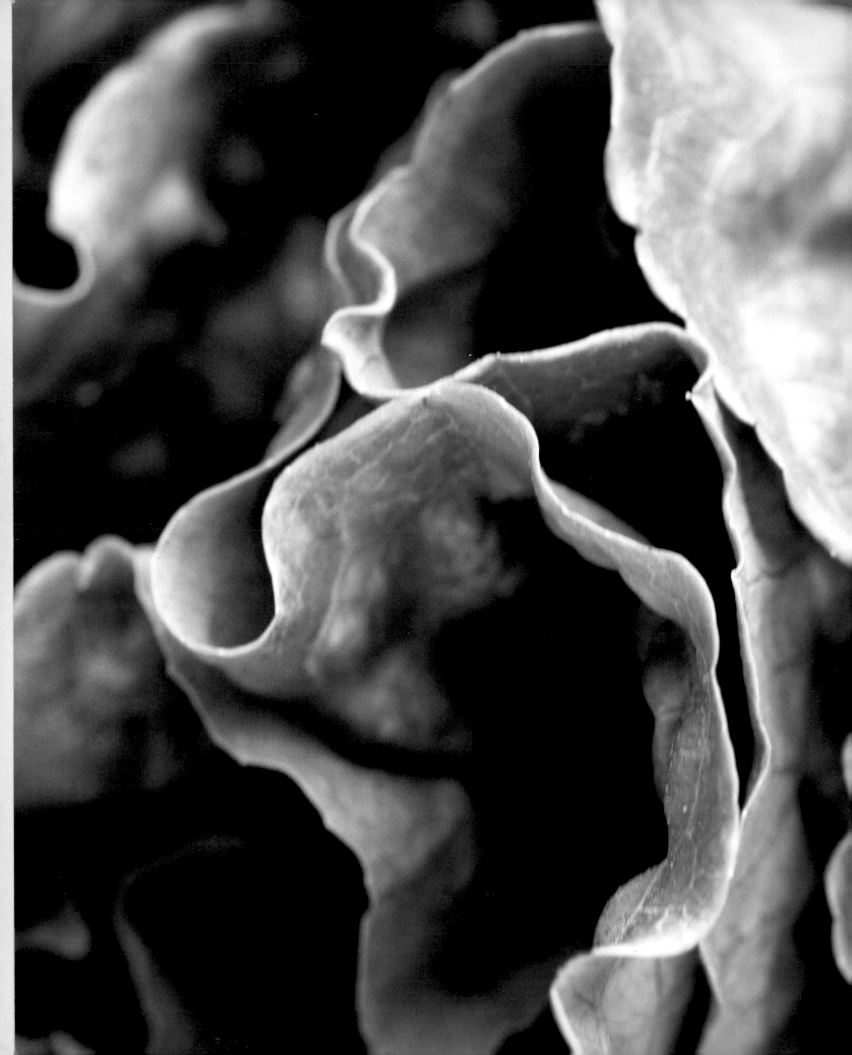

CHAPTER 2

Afternoon

Lavender Lemonade

I was first introduced to this drink by my friend Kent at the Ruby Ranch in New Mexico. He and my best friend, Bob, had planted an entire field of lavender and it seemed they were trying to find as many ways to use it as humanly possible. I helped harvest the lavender one summer and slept in the drying room below racks of freshly cut blossoms. (Maybe I was hallucinating from a lavender overdose, but I dreamed I was in an E. M. Forster novel.) This drink is extremely elegant, yet also very easy to make. The most exciting part is watching the alchemy as you stir the fragrant lavender infusion into the yellow lemonade: it turns bright pink right before your eyes!

{ **SERVES 8** }

¼ **cup dried lavender flowers**

1½ **cups boiling water**

One **12-ounce can frozen lemonade concentrate, thawed**

5 **cups cold filtered water**
  Ice cubes

In a heatproof pitcher or teapot, combine the lavender and boiling water. Cover and let steep for 10 minutes. Strain, discarding the lavender, and let cool completely.

In a 2-quart pitcher, combine the lemonade concentrate and cold filtered water and stir until well mixed. Stir in the lavender infusion. Serve over ice.

Shandy

My friend Bob, whose kin hail from Australia, says the women in his family drink shandy, a beer-based spritzer, as a way of keeping up with the blokes, who favored stronger quaffs. Although the shandy probably originated as a way of creating a "lite" beer before such things existed, this concoction is incredibly refreshing on a hot summer day no matter what your motivation. Here, I call for either a hefeweizen, which is a German style of beer that has a lemony bite yet isn't too bitter, or a pilsner, which is a pale lager with a bit more of the taste of hops. However, this simple recipe invites experimentation with the proportions and ingredients, so dive right in!

{ **SERVES 2** }

One 12-ounce bottle hefeweizen or pilsner

12 ounces lemon-lime soda or Ginger Beer (page 63)

Chill two lager glasses in the freezer for at least 10 minutes.

Pour 6 ounces of beer into each, followed by the soda. Stir gently and serve right away.

Ginger Beer

There is nothing quite like the zing of ginger beer made from fresh gingerroot. This version contains no alcohol, so those of you itching for a buzz will need to add a shot of vodka to make it a Moscow Mule. Be sure to follow the directions exactly, and also be sure to use filtered water, as the chlorine in tap water can kill the yeast. Since this recipe calls for quite a bit of freshly squeezed lemon juice, here's a tip to help maximize the amount you get from each lemon: bring the lemons to room temperature before squeezing. As you gain experience in bottling your own ginger beer, feel free to play with the recipe, adjusting the proportions of lemon juice, sugar, and ginger. One important note: You'll need twelve 16-ounce flip-top bottles for this recipe, so be sure to have those on hand before you begin. If you drink Grolsch beer, this is a great way to repurpose those bottles. Whatever type of bottles you use, be sure to sterilize them before filling.

···{ **MAKES TWELVE 16-OUNCE BOTTLES** }···

4 **cups sugar**

4 **cups filtered, unchlorinated water, plus 15 cups warm filtered, unchlorinated water (97°F to 102°F)**

3 **cups fresh lemon juice (from about 20 lemons)**

1¼ **pounds fresh ginger**

¾ **teaspoon champagne yeast, such as Premier Cuvée, or baking yeast**

In a large saucepan, combine the sugar and the 4 cups water. Bring to a boil over medium-high heat, stirring until the sugar dissolves. Remove from the heat and let cool.

Strain the lemon juice through cheesecloth or a fine-mesh sieve, discarding the pulp and seeds.

Peel the ginger, then finely grate it. Put the ginger on three layers of cheesecloth, then gather it into a bundle, hold it over a bowl, and twist or press the cheesecloth to extract the ginger juice. Alternatively, use a masticating juice extractor, such as a Champion or Hurom juicer, to extract the ginger juice. You should end up with about 12 ounces of ginger juice.

CONTINUED

In a pitcher or other container large enough to accommodate 1½ gallons of liquid, combine the sugar syrup, lemon juice, ginger juice, and 15 cups warm water and stir until well mixed. Add the yeast and stir until dissolved.

Using a funnel, fill twelve 16-ounce flip-top bottles with the mixture, leaving 1 to 1½ inches of headroom in each bottle, then seal the cap. Store the bottles in a warm place (70°F to 80°F), completely away from light, for exactly 48 hours (see Tip). Refrigerate immediately to stop the fermentation process.

Once the ginger beer is chilled, open the top very slowly while pressing down on it with a dishcloth; this will allow the carbon dioxide to escape gradually, rather than spouting like a geyser when serving.

TIP: Until you've made this recipe a few times, follow the directions exactly. Don't let your ginger beer ferment for more than 48 hours or some of the bottles might burst due to overproduction of carbon dioxide. If you're concerned about this, put the bottles in a closed ice chest while they're fermenting as a precaution.

Dukkah
WITH RUSTIC BREAD

Dukkah, a coarse, dry, dipping powder, is an exotic condiment that doesn't really fit into any of the usual culinary categories. Traditionally, this Egyptian medley of toasted nuts and spices is sold in paper cones, accompanied with fresh bread. The bread is first dipped into a bowl of your best-quality olive oil, then in the *dukkah*. I recommend serving it as an appetizer or, accompanied by a glass of crisp white wine and some fresh in-season fruit, as a midafternoon snack. The blend can also be used as a garnish on soups or salads. One of the key flavors in this recipe is sumac. Though you need only a small amount, hunting down the gorgeous reddish purple powder made from sour, astringent sumac fruits is well worth the effort. That said, you can omit the sumac and still enjoy *dukkah*.

······························{ **MAKES 1½ CUPS OF DUKKAH; SERVES ABOUT 6** }······························

⅓ cup shelled raw pistachios

⅓ cup raw almonds

⅓ cup raw hazelnuts

¾ cup sesame seeds

¼ cup coriander seeds

1½ tablespoons cumin seeds

1 tablespoon fennel seeds

1 tablespoon yellow mustard seeds

1 tablespoon ground sumac

½ teaspoon salt

⅛ teaspoon freshly ground pepper

1 loaf rustic bread, preferably Twenty-One-Hour Boule (page 47)

Extra-virgin olive oil for dipping

CONTINUED

Preheat the oven to 350°F.

Spread the pistachios, almonds, and hazelnuts in a single layer on a rimmed baking sheet and bake for 10 to 15 minutes, until lightly toasted and fragrant, stirring once about halfway through baking. Let cool for 5 to 10 minutes, then coarsely chop the nuts.

In a dry, heavy skillet, toast the sesame seeds over medium heat until fragrant, about 2 minutes. Transfer the sesame seeds to a plate to cool. Repeat, toasting the coriander seeds, cumin seeds, fennel seeds, and mustard seeds separately in the skillet until fragrant.

Once the seeds have cooled, put them in a food processor. Add the sumac and chopped nuts and pulse until coarsely ground. Add the salt and pepper and pulse a time or two to combine.

Slice the bread, then cut each slice in half or into large cubes. Pour some olive oil into a shallow bowl. Gather around and dip the bread in the olive oil and then in the *dukkah*.

Store the *dukkah* in an airtight container in a cool place; it will keep for up to 1 month.

Muhammara

This voluptuous, crimson spread is common throughout the Middle East but still relatively rare in the West. It's an aromatic mixture made from nuts, roasted red bell peppers, pomegranate molasses (a reduction of pomegranate juice yielding a thick, tart syrup), and Aleppo pepper (a bright-red mild chile pepper native to Syria). *Muhammara* is delicious as a dip, as a spread on sandwiches, or simply enjoyed on crackers or slice of bread.

······························· { **MAKES 2 CUPS; SERVES ABOUT 6** } ·······························

½ **cup raw walnuts (2 ounces)**

¼ **cup raw pine nuts (1 ounce)**

3 **red bell peppers or jarred roasted red bell peppers, drained**

¾ **cup dried bread crumbs**

4 **garlic cloves, coarsely chopped**

1 **tablespoon pomegranate molasses**

3 **tablespoons fresh lemon juice**

1 **tablespoon Aleppo pepper (see Tip)**

1 **teaspoon ground cumin**

⅓ **cup extra-virgin olive oil**

Salt

Freshly ground pepper

Sliced rustic bread, preferably Twenty-One-Hour Boule (page 47), or pita chips

In a dry, heavy skillet over medium heat, toast the walnuts and pine nuts, shaking the pan frequently, until fragrant, about 5 minutes.

If using fresh bell peppers, roast them over a medium to high gas flame on either the stovetop or an outdoor grill. Use tongs to turn the peppers repeatedly until most of the skin is charred, blackened, and slightly blistered. Be careful not to overcook the peppers, or they may split and be difficult to peel. Put them in a heatproof bowl and cover with a plate or plastic wrap to allow them to steam.

When the roasted peppers are cool enough to handle, gently peel away the skin using your fingers or a small paring knife. Resist the urge to run the peppers under water, as this will remove their nice smoky flavor. Remove and discard the core and seeds.

CONTINUED

In a food processor, combine the roasted peppers, nuts, bread crumbs, garlic, pomegranate molasses, lemon juice, Aleppo pepper, and cumin. Process until smooth, stopping to scrape down the sides of the food processor bowl if necessary. Add the olive oil and process until smooth, about 30 seconds. Season with salt and pepper and pulse once more to combine.

Transfer to a serving bowl and serve with the bread alongside for dipping.

TIP: If you don't have Aleppo pepper on hand, you can substitute 2 teaspoons of smoked Spanish paprika combined with 1 teaspoon of ground cayenne pepper.

Hummus
WITH TAHINI

Although you can now find packaged, premade hummus in practically any grocery store, it's well worth making your own from scratch (just note that the beans require a soaking overnight before being cooked). The vivid flavors here remind me of the authentic version served at one of the few Middle Eastern restaurants in Southern California in the 1960s. My mother loved ethnic food, and we were regulars at Kabakian's, an Armenian restaurant owned by the aging, eponymous Kabakian brothers. If you ordered *hummus bi tahina* (which simply means "garbanzo beans with sesame paste"), the brothers would shuffle over to your table in their slippers, pushing a cart with a plate of hummus and a basket of freshly baked pita bread. Then, determined to show you how to eat properly in the style of their homeland, they would tear off a piece of pita, dip it into your plate of hummus, and then actually stick it in your mouth! Now that's service.

MAKES 4 CUPS; SERVES ABOUT 8

8 ounces dried garbanzo beans

1 tablespoon baking soda

5 garlic cloves

¼ cup fresh lemon juice

½ cup tahini

½ cup extra-virgin olive oil, plus more for garnish

1 teaspoon ground cumin

1 teaspoon salt

Paprika for garnish

Ground sumac for garnish

Warm pita bread for serving

In a medium bowl, combine the garbanzo beans and baking soda. Pour water into the bowl until the beans are covered by 1 inch and let soak for at least 8 hours and up to overnight in the refrigerator.

Drain and rinse the beans, put them in a medium saucepan, and add fresh water to cover by 2 inches. Bring to a boil over high heat, then lower the heat, cover, and simmer until the beans are tender, 30 to 40 minutes.

CONTINUED

Drain the beans, reserving their cooking liquid. Set aside about a dozen whole garbanzos. In a food processor or blender, combine the remaining beans with the garlic, lemon juice, tahini, olive oil, cumin, salt, and ¼ cup of the cooking liquid. Process until smooth, about 1 minute.

Transfer the hummus to a shallow serving bowl. With the back of a large tablespoon, make an indentation in the center of the hummus and drizzle in a bit of olive oil. Dust the top with paprika and sumac, then scatter the reserved whole garbanzos over the top. Serve with the warm pita bread. Wearing slippers while serving is optional, but it's a nice touch.

Three Salsas
WITH HOMEMADE TORTILLA CHIPS

Not being satisfied with merely one salsa recipe, I've gone overboard and given you three. The only thing missing is a batch of Blood Orange Margaritas (page 114). Two of these salsa recipes call for varieties of dried chiles that may be unfamiliar. You can find them at most Latin American grocery stores and online. They are well worth the search, as each has its own distinct personality, flavor, and heat. Guajillos are a mild, reddish brown chile; árbols are thin, small chiles with a bit more heat; and chipotle moras are dried, smoked jalapeños and pack the most heat of the three. A word of advice to the chile novice: Don't touch your face or any delicate areas of your body with your hands while working with the chiles. You may want to wear a pair of disposable gloves or just be sure to wash your hands thoroughly with soap and water afterward.

{ **SERVES 6 TO 8** }

Salsa Roja

3 garlic cloves, unpeeled
1 large serrano chile, stemmed
2 large tomatoes
1 tablespoon minced fresh cilantro
1 teaspoon salt
¼ teaspoon sugar

Preheat the broiler.

In a dry, heavy skillet over medium heat, toast the garlic and serrano, turning constantly, until browned and fragrant, about 10 minutes. When cool enough to handle, peel the garlic and trim and discard the serrano stem.

Put the tomatoes in a small ovenproof pan and broil, turning a couple of times, for 10 to 15 minutes, until their skins split and they're evenly charred. When cool enough to handle, cut out and discard the cores.

In a blender, combine the garlic and serrano and chop with quick pulses. Add the tomatoes, cilantro, salt, and sugar and blend until smooth. Transfer to a bowl and let cool before serving.

Salsa Negra

4 tablespoons canola oil

3 ounces dried chipotle mora chiles

11 garlic cloves, peeled

2 cups water

½ teaspoon salt

In a heavy skillet, heat 2 tablespoons of the canola oil over medium heat. Add the chiles and garlic and cook, stirring constantly, until the chiles puff up and the garlic has browned, about 5 minutes.

Put the chiles in a bowl and add hot water to cover. Let soak until soft, 20 to 30 minutes.

Drain the chiles, then remove their stems and seeds. In a blender, combine the chiles, garlic, and the 2 cups water and blend until smooth.

In the same skillet, heat the remaining 2 tablespoons oil over medium heat. Carefully pour in the blended mixture and cook, stirring constantly, for 15 minutes. Stir in the salt, then transfer to a bowl and let cool before serving.

Guajillo and Chile de Árbol Salsa

3 or 4 guajillo chiles

1 or 2 chiles de árbol

8 ounces tomatillos, husked and rinsed

½ cup chopped yellow onion (about 1 small onion)

1 garlic clove, coarsely chopped

1 teaspoon salt

1 tablespoon minced fresh cilantro

Rinse the guajillos and chiles de árbol, then pat them dry. In a dry, heavy skillet over medium heat, toast the chiles, turning constantly, until fragrant, about 3 minutes.

Put the tomatillos in a medium saucepan and add water to cover. Bring to a boil over high heat, then lower the heat and simmer for 5 minutes. Use a slotted spoon to transfer the tomatillos from their cooking water to a blender.

Put the toasted chiles in the cooking water and rehydrate for 10 to 15 minutes. Drain the chiles, then remove their stems and seeds. Put the chiles, onion, garlic, salt, and cilantro in the blender with the tomatillos and blend until smooth. Transfer to a bowl and let cool before serving.

CONTINUED

Tortilla Chips

6 to 12 corn tortillas
Canola oil for frying
Salt

Stack the tortillas and cut them in half cross-wise. Cut each stack of halves into thirds, creating six triangular wedges per tortilla.

In a deep, heavy pot, heat 2 to 3 inches of canola oil over medium-high heat until it registers 375°F on a deep-frying thermometer.

Drop a handful of tortillas at a time into the hot oil and fry until golden brown, 1 to 2 minutes, turning if necessary. Be sure not to fry too many chips at a time; leave enough room in the pot for them to move about freely so they'll brown evenly.

Remove the cooked chips with a slotted spoon and drain on paper towels. Sprinkle with salt and serve warm.

Ceviche de Vegan

My hope is that this lovely dish will conjure up a vision of an open-air shack on a warm beach. White plastic chairs and mismatched tables covered with slick, hibiscus-patterned oilcloth dot the white sand. There's a salty waft of sea air inflecting each bite of this dish. Although ceviche is, strictly speaking, a seafood cocktail, this all-vegetable version employs the traditional fresh lime juice to "cook" the ingredients and provide a tart, acidic dressing. Serve the ceviche in clear glass bowls or glasses to showcase the gorgeous colors of the ingredients. *Vamos a la playa!*

{ **SERVES** 4 }

4 ounces new potatoes, peeled and cut into ½-inch dice

1¼ teaspoons salt

1 jalapeño pepper, seeded and minced

½ red bell pepper, seeded, deribbed, and cut into ¼-inch dice

½ yellow bell pepper, seeded, deribbed, and cut into ¼-inch dice

½ medium red onion, thinly sliced

1 garlic clove, minced

½ cup green olives, pitted and halved

1 cup small cherry tomatoes, halved, or 10 ounces sun-dried tomatoes packed in olive oil, drained and coarsely chopped

1 to 2 Persian cucumbers, unpeeled, cut into ½-inch dice (about ½ cup). If Persian cucumbers aren't available, substitute a hothouse variety.

¼ cup coarsely chopped fresh cilantro

1 cup fresh lime juice

1 tablespoon extra-virgin olive oil

⅛ teaspoon ground cumin

1 ripe avocado, cut into ½-inch dice

CONTINUED

Put the potatoes in a medium saucepan and add cold water to cover by 2 inches. Add 1 teaspoon of the salt and bring to a boil over high heat. Lower the heat, cover, and simmer until the potatoes give easily when pierced with the tip of a sharp knife, 8 to 10 minutes. Be careful not to overcook them; they should still be firm enough to hold their shape well.

In a large bowl, combine the warm potatoes with the jalapeño, bell peppers, onion, garlic, olives, tomatoes, cucumber, and cilantro.

In a small bowl, combine the lime juice, olive oil, cumin, and remaining ¼ teaspoon salt and stir until well mixed. Pour the mixture over the vegetables and stir gently until all of the vegetables are evenly coated, being careful not to break up the cubes of potato. Add the avocado and stir gently to combine. Serve right away at room temperature, or refrigerate for up to 3 days and bring to room temperature before serving.

Jicama Salad

I call jicama "the tofu of the tuber world." With its pristine white color and mild flavor, it mirrors tofu's versatility, easily playing host to strong-flavored ingredients. Here, jalapeño and chipotle give the dish a kick, balancing out the jicama's moist, refreshing crunch. The salad gets its beautiful green color from green onions and cilantro whirled into a thick, creamy dressing similar to green goddess.

{ SERVES 4 }

DRESSING

- 6 to 8 green onions (white and green parts), coarsely chopped
- 1 bunch fresh cilantro, stemmed and coarsely chopped
- 1 jalapeño pepper, seeded and coarsely chopped
- 1 cup vegan mayonnaise, preferably Vegenaise brand
- Juice of 2 limes
- 1 chipotle chile in adobo sauce
- 1 teaspoon salt
- Freshly ground pepper

- 1 large jicama
- Cilantro sprigs for garnish

TO MAKE THE DRESSING: In a food processor, combine the green onions, cilantro, jalapeño, mayonnaise, lime juice, chipotle chile, and salt and process until smooth. Season with pepper.

Peel the jicama and cut it in half. Cut each half into ⅛-inch slices. Working with stacks of a few slices at a time, cut the jicama lengthwise into ⅛-inch-thick matchsticks, then crosswise into ⅛-inch dice. Put the jicama in a large bowl.

Add the dressing to the jicama and stir until well mixed. Refrigerate for 20 to 30 minutes to allow the flavors to meld. Serve garnished with the cilantro sprigs.

Fava Bean Salad

Fava beans are known by many names, including broad beans, field beans, and Windsor beans. But whatever you call them, they are a harbinger of spring, with a welcome, slightly bitter taste that's somewhat reminiscent of green peas. The shucking and peeling required to actually get to the beans might seem laborious, but that's what guests are for! Ply your helpers with a Shandy (page 61) and put on an obscure Algerian rai CD, and I bet you won't hear one complaint.

{ **SERVES 4** }

DRESSING

- 1 **garlic clove, minced**
- 1 **tablespoon extra-virgin olive oil**
- 3 **tablespoons red wine vinegar**
- 1 **tablespoon fresh lemon juice**
- 1 **teaspoon salt**
- ½ **teaspoon Aleppo pepper or red pepper flakes**
- **Freshly ground pepper**

SALAD

- 3 **pounds fresh fava beans in the shell**
- 2 **cups corn kernels (from 2 to 3 ears of corn)**
- 1 **red bell pepper, seeded, deribbed, and cut into ¼-inch dice**
- 1 **medium cucumber, peeled, quartered lengthwise, and thinly sliced**
- ½ **medium red onion, thinly sliced**
- 3 **tablespoons chopped fresh flat-leaf parsley**
- ¾ **cup pine nuts (3 ounces), toasted (see Tip, page 101)**

TO MAKE THE DRESSING: In a small bowl, combine the garlic, olive oil, vinegar, lemon juice, salt, and Aleppo pepper. Season with pepper and stir until well mixed.

TO MAKE THE SALAD: Prepare an ice-water bath by filling a large bowl with ice and water.

Bring a large pot of water to a boil. Add the fava beans and cook for 2 minutes, then transfer to the ice-water bath with a slotted spoon. Return the water to a boil, then add the corn. Boil for 1 minute, then drain.

When the beans are cool enough to handle, peel off and discard the shells. In a large serving bowl, combine the shucked beans, corn, bell pepper, cucumber, onion, parsley, and pine nuts and stir until well mixed. Add the dressing and toss until the vegetables are evenly coated. Serve right away at room temperature.

Tofu Caprese Stack

This gorgeous salad is a towering homage to Caprese salad, a dish from the Italian island of Capri that traditionally uses fresh mozzarella. The green of the basil, red of the tomato, and white of the tofu (sitting in for the mozzarella) are said to represent the colors of Italy's flag. Although the recipe calls for extra-firm tofu, firm tofu also works well here. Only make this salad in summer and early autumn, as the key to success is using the ripest tomatoes and freshest basil leaves possible! I'm indebted to my sister-in-law, Wendy, for the dressing used here, and her brilliant idea of replacing the typical lemon juice with lime juice. It's so simple and tasty that I can't see why you would ever need to buy bottled vinaigrette again.

SERVES 6

3 large tomatoes, preferably heirloom

1¾ pounds extra-firm tofu, drained

24 large fresh basil leaves
Wendy's Vinaigrette (page 86)

Cut each tomato into six slices. Place one slice each in the center of six individual serving plates. Pat the tofu lightly with a paper towel or clean kitchen towel to remove excess moisture. Cut each block into ¼-inch slices (you should have about twelve slices altogether). Use a 3-inch round biscuit cutter to cut twelve circles from the tofu slices, reserving the scraps for another use. Top each slice of tomato with a basil leaf and a tofu round. Drizzle one-third of the vinaigrette over the tofu, dividing it evenly among the plates. Place a basil leaf on top of each disk of tofu. Repeat the layers, stacking with another tomato slice and tofu disk, drizzling another one-third of the vinaigrette over the tofu, and topping with a basil leaf. Top each stack with another tomato slice and a final basil leaf, then drizzle with the remaining vinaigrette. Serve right away.

Wendy's Vinaigrette

[**MAKES ABOUT ⅓ CUP**]

Juice of ½ lime
1 **teaspoon balsamic vinegar**
2 **teaspoons Dijon mustard**
1 **small shallot, minced**
½ **teaspoon Veganshire Sauce (page 38, optional)**
3 **tablespoons extra-virgin olive oil**
Salt
Freshly ground pepper

In a small bowl, combine the lime juice, vinegar, mustard, shallot, and Veganshire Sauce (if using) and whisk together. Slowly add the olive oil in a thin stream, whisking constantly until smooth and emulsified. Season with salt and pepper. Store, tightly covered, in the refrigerator for up to 1 week.

Roasted Pepper Involtini

Involtini means "stuffed and rolled" in Italian. This beautiful method of preparing multicolored bell peppers results in a dish that can be offered as an appetizer or served as part of an antipasto plate. The fresh bay leaves are really for visual effect, but they do impart a nice earthy fragrance to the peppers. If you can't find fresh bay leaves, use dried bay leaves when marinating the peppers. For presentation purposes, you can line the platter with drained grape leaves packed in brine if you like.

{ **SERVES 6** }

2 **large red bell peppers**

2 **large yellow or orange bell peppers**

10 **fresh or dried bay leaves**

8 **ounces extra-firm tofu, drained**

2 **tablespoons nutritional yeast flakes**

1 **garlic clove**

1 **teaspoon fresh lemon juice**

1 **teaspoon extra-virgin olive oil**

½ **teaspoon salt**

2 **grinds of pepper**

2 **plum tomatoes, peeled and seeded (see Tip, page 95) and finely diced**

8 **fresh basil leaves, plus thinly sliced or torn basil leaves for garnish**

Roast the bell peppers over a medium to high gas flame on either the stovetop or an outdoor grill. Use tongs to turn the peppers repeatedly until most of the skin is charred, blackened, and slightly blistered. Be careful not to over-cook the peppers, or they may split and be difficult to peel. Put them in a heatproof bowl and cover with a plate or plastic wrap to allow them to steam.

When the roasted peppers are cool enough to handle, gently peel away the skin using your fingers or a small paring knife. Resist the urge to run the peppers under water, as this will remove their nice smoky flavor. Put the peeled peppers back in the bowl. Add the bay leaves to the bowl, toss gently, and allow to infuse for 1 hour.

CONTINUED

In a food processor, combine the tofu, nutritional yeast, garlic, lemon juice, olive oil, salt, and pepper and process until the mixture is thick and smooth. Gently fold in the tomatoes.

Put the peppers on a work surface, remove the stems, and butterfly the peppers in half lengthwise to form one flat surface. Remove the seeds. Lay the pepper halves out flat and place 2 basil leaves on each, then top with 2 tablespoons of the tofu mixture. Roll each pepper into a cylinder and lay them, seam-side down, onto a platter. Refrigerate for 20 minutes, then cut the rolls into thick slices.

To serve, line a platter with the reserved bay leaves. Arrange the involtini on top of the bay leaves, flat-side down, and garnish with the thinly sliced basil.

Summer Rolls

WITH TWO DIPPING SAUCES

These beautiful rolls are vegan relatives of their traditional Vietnamese cousins. With their crisp vegetables, cool mint, and smooth rice paper wrappers, they're particularly refreshing in the summer months, but they are truly delicious any time of year. Personally, I'm never satisfied with only one dipping sauce, so I've included two. If you're anything like me, you'll enjoy not being able to decide which one you prefer.

{ **SERVES 4** }

Twelve 8½-inch round rice paper spring roll wrappers

12 red leaf lettuce leaves, cut in half lengthwise, plus more for serving

4 medium carrots, peeled and cut into matchsticks

1 red bell pepper, seeded, deribbed, and cut into matchsticks

½ seedless cucumber, peeled and cut into matchsticks

1 bunch fresh mint, trimmed

1 bunch fresh cilantro, trimmed

1 bunch green onions, cut lengthwise into thin strips

Peanut Dipping Sauce (page 92) for serving

Soy Dipping Sauce (page 92) for serving

Fill a pan or wide, shallow bowl large enough to hold the rice paper with hot water. Lightly dampen a clean kitchen towel and spread it on a clean surface. Dip a sheet of rice paper in the hot water for 5 seconds, then transfer to the dampened towel and smooth it out; the wrapper will still feel hard but will soften as it sits.

Lay a piece of lettuce on the bottom third of the rice paper. Top the lettuce with about one-twelfth of the carrots, bell pepper, cucumber, mint, and cilantro. Roll the wrapper up halfway to enclose the fillings and tuck in the ends. Place a few green onion strips on the roll and continue to roll so the green onions are enclosed but still show through the wrapper.

Cover a serving platter with more lettuce leaves. Put the finished roll on the platter and cover with a damp paper towel. Continue filling and rolling the remaining wrappers in the same way. Serve on a bed of lettuce leaves, with the dipping sauces alongside.

Peanut Dipping Sauce

{ MAKES 1½ CUPS }

1 tablespoon light sesame oil

1 small shallot, finely chopped

1 garlic clove, minced

½ jalapeño pepper, minced (seeded if you prefer a milder heat level)

½ cup unsalted smooth peanut butter

¾ cup vegetable stock, preferably homemade (page 98)

1 tablespoon Veganshire Sauce (page 38)

¾ teaspoon agave syrup

1 tablespoon fresh lime juice

1 teaspoon toasted sesame oil

Chopped roasted peanuts for garnish

In a small saucepan, heat the light sesame oil over medium heat. Add the shallot, garlic, and jalapeño and sauté until beginning to brown, about 4 minutes. Stir in the peanut butter, stock, Veganshire Sauce, and agave syrup and simmer, stirring occasionally, for 5 minutes. Let cool slightly.

Pour the mixture into a blender, blend until smooth, adding a bit of water if the sauce is too thick. Transfer to a serving bowl and stir in the lime juice and toasted sesame oil. Sprinkle with the chopped peanuts before serving.

Soy Dipping Sauce

{ MAKES ABOUT ½ CUP }

¼ cup soy sauce

¼ cup rice wine vinegar

1 tablespoon thinly sliced scallions (white and green parts)

In a small bowl, combine the soy sauce, vinegar, and scallions and stir until well mixed. Serve immediately.

Baked Ratatouille

IN PHYLLO

Ratatouille, the darling of dinner parties in the 1970s, stages a comeback. In this updated version, France meets Greece as savory eggplant, zucchini, and tomatoes are sandwiched between layers of flaky phyllo dough. Phyllo (sometimes spelled filo) is the delicate, paper-thin dough commonly used in Middle Eastern desserts such as baklava, but it's also a natural for savory dishes such as this.

SERVES 6 TO 8

6 tablespoons extra-virgin olive oil, or as needed

1 medium yellow onion, halved and thinly sliced

4 garlic cloves, minced

1 large eggplant, unpeeled, cut into ½-inch dice

3 medium zucchini, cut into ½-inch dice

1½ pounds plum tomatoes, peeled and seeded (see Tip) and cut into ½-inch dice

1 teaspoon salt

½ teaspoon freshly ground pepper

½ cup finely chopped fresh parsley

¼ cup finely chopped fresh dill

Twelve 12-by-17-inch phyllo sheets, thawed if frozen

In a large skillet, heat 3 tablespoons of the olive oil over medium heat. Add the onion and sauté until translucent, about 5 minutes. Add the garlic and sauté for 30 seconds. Add the eggplant and zucchini and sauté until all of the vegetables are tender, about 10 minutes. Stir in the tomatoes, salt, and pepper; lower the heat; and simmer, stirring occasionally, until most of the liquid has evaporated, 5 to 8 minutes. Stir in the parsley and dill and remove from the heat.

Position a rack in the middle of the oven and preheat the oven to 425°F. Coat a 9-by-13-inch baking pan with some of the remaining olive oil.

CONTINUED

Unroll the phyllo and trim the sheets to just fit inside the pan, then cover with plastic wrap and a damp kitchen towel to keep them from drying out. Keeping the remaining sheets covered, put one sheet on a clean work surface and use a pastry brush to gently coat with some of the remaining olive oil. Put a second sheet on top and brush with more olive oil. Repeat until you have a stack of six sheets brushed with olive oil. Set aside and repeat, creating a second stack of six sheets brushed with olive oil.

Carefully transfer one of the phyllo stacks into the prepared pan and spoon the vegetables on top, spreading the mixture in an even layer. Cover with the second stack of phyllo sheets. Brush the top sheet of phyllo with a bit more olive oil.

Bake for about 20 minutes, until the top is golden brown. Remove from the oven and let sit for 5 minutes. Use a sharp knife to cut the pastry into squares. Serve right away.

TIP: To seed the tomatoes, bring a large saucepan of water to a boil. Score a small X in the bottom of each tomato with a knife. Put the tomatoes in the boiling water and blanch for 1 minute. Remove them with a slotted spoon. When cool enough to handle, slip off the skins, cut the tomatoes in half, and scoop out seeds.

Garbanzo Bean and Tomato Soup

I wanted to call this recipe "Zuppa di Ceci con Pomodori," but my copy editor insisted that it be in English. But doesn't it sound better in Italian? For optimum flavor, use dried beans to make this hearty dish. However, the beans do require overnight soaking before being cooked, so in a pinch you can use canned garbanzos. Orzo is a small, rice-shaped pasta that lends itself well to this soup, but feel free to substitute any pasta you happen to have on hand.

{ **SERVES 4 TO 6** }

1¼ **cups dried garbanzo beans, or two 15-ounce cans, drained**

6 **cups vegetable stock, preferably homemade (see page 98)**

1 **cup orzo**

One **28-ounce can crushed or diced tomatoes**

1 **tablespoon extra-virgin olive oil, plus more for drizzling**

4 **garlic cloves, minced**

2 **teaspoons chopped fresh rosemary**

1 **teaspoon chopped fresh thyme**

1 **teaspoon salt**

½ **teaspoon freshly ground pepper**

If using dried garbanzo beans, put them in a large bowl and add water to cover by at least 2 inches. Let soak for at least 8 hours and up to overnight.

Drain and rinse the beans, put them in a large soup pot or stockpot, and add fresh water to cover by 2 inches. Bring to a boil over high heat, then lower the heat, cover, and simmer, stirring occasionally, for about 2 hours, until tender. Drain and set aside.

In the same pot, bring the stock to a boil over high heat. Lower the heat to medium-high, add the orzo, and cook until al dente, about 10 minutes. Stir in the garbanzos and tomatoes and bring the soup back to a simmer.

Meanwhile, in a small skillet, heat the olive oil over medium heat. Add the garlic, rosemary, and thyme and sauté until fragrant, about 30 seconds. Stir the seasonings into the beans, along with the salt and pepper.

Transfer 2 cups of the soup to a blender or food processor and blend until smooth. Return the purée to the pot. Taste and adjust the seasoning. Serve the soup in warmed bowls with a drizzle of olive oil on top.

Vegetable Stock

2 **tablespoons olive oil**

3 **onions, sliced**

2 **carrots, sliced**

2 **celery stalks, sliced**

2 **parsnips, sliced**

6 **cloves garlic, sliced**

2 **bay leaves**

1 **teaspoon whole black peppercorns**

6 **sprigs parsley**

2 **teaspoons fresh rosemary**

2 **teaspoons fresh thyme**

4 **quarts water**

In a large pot, heat the olive oil over medium heat. Add the onions, carrots, celery, parsnips, and garlic and sauté until the onions are translucent and the rest of the vegetables have softened, about 10 minutes. Stir in the bay leaves, peppercorns, parsley, rosemary, thyme and water. Lower the heat and simmer for 2 hours. Strain, discarding the solids.

Cool before storing in the refrigerator for up to 3 days or in the freezer for up to 1 month.

TIP: I like to save vegetable trimmings such as potato peelings, mushroom stems, carrot tops, leek trimmings or chard ribs and add a few handfuls of them to the pot when you add the water. Also consider freezing your trimmings until you are ready to make a batch of broth. Just add them in thawed or frozen.

Broiled Tofu, Carrots, and Shiitake Mushrooms

From the title of this recipe, you may think it's going to be a lot like your Auntie Sunflower's hippie stir-fry, but it's not. The preparation methods used here owe more to Japanese Zen temple cookery than to Woodstock. Here, tofu, carrots, and shiitake mushrooms are broiled rather than stir-fried. This lighter touch makes room for the flavors of ginger and sesame to find enlightenment.

{ **SERVES 4** }

1½ **pounds carrots**

1¾ **pounds extra-firm tofu, drained and pressed (see Tip, page 166)**

3 **ounces shiitake mushrooms, stemmed**

¼ **cup peanut oil**

¼ **cup soy sauce**

1 **teaspoon salt**

1 **tablespoon grated peeled fresh ginger**

5 **green onions, thinly sliced (white and green parts)**

2 **tablespoons rice vinegar**

1 **tablespoon toasted sesame oil**

1 **tablespoon sesame seeds, toasted (see Tip), for garnish**

Set an oven rack 4 to 5 inches below the broiler and preheat the broiler. Line a rimmed baking sheet with foil.

Cut the carrots crosswise into 3-inch lengths. Depending on the thickness of the carrots, cut the pieces lengthwise to a width of about ½ inch. Cut the tofu into 1½-inch dice. Thinly slice the mushrooms.

In a large bowl, combine the peanut oil, soy sauce, salt, and ginger. Add the mushrooms and gently toss until evenly coated with the marinade. Transfer the mushrooms to the prepared baking sheet. Put the tofu in the bowl with the remaining marinade and toss to evenly coat.

CONTINUED

Broil the mushrooms for 5 to 10 minutes, until tender, turning once about halfway through. Keep an eye on them so they don't burn. Transfer the mushrooms to a bowl and cover to keep warm. Leave the oven on.

Add the carrots to the bowl of tofu and toss to evenly coat. Transfer the carrots and tofu to the same baking sheet, reserving the marinade.

Broil the carrots and tofu for 20 to 30 minutes, until nicely browned, turning a time or two as needed. Keep an eye on them so they don't burn. When done, transfer to the bowl of reserved marinade. Add the mushrooms, green onions, vinegar, and sesame oil and toss gently until evenly coated. Transfer to a large platter or smaller individual dishes and sprinkle with the toasted sesame seeds before serving.

TIP: To toast sesame seeds, as well as pine nuts, pistachios, walnuts, coconut, and other nuts and seeds, put them in a dry, heavy skillet over medium heat and cook, shaking the pan frequently, until fragrant and just beginning to color. For sesame seeds, that's usually just 1 or 2 minutes. Keep a close eye on them, as they can burn quickly. When cooking larger quantities or larger seeds and nuts, the toasting time will be lengthier, but it's still essential to watch them closely.

Sweet Crema
WITH BERRIES AND CHAMBORD

Lighter than an English trifle (or for that matter, an American parfait), this is one of those desserts that is refreshing rather than rich. There are only three simple components: a sweet cashew crema; fresh berries; and a deep, dark, syrupy raspberry sauce.

······················ { **SERVES 4** } ······················

SWEET CASHEW CREMA

- ¾ cup raw cashew pieces (4 ounces)
- 8 ounces extra-firm tofu, drained
- ¼ cup agave syrup
- 2 tablespoons fresh lemon juice
- 1 tablespoon Cognac
- 1 tablespoon canola oil
- 1 teaspoon pure vanilla extract
- ½ teaspoon sea salt

- ½ cup Chambord or other raspberry liqueur
- 1½ cups fresh blackberries or raspberries, or 10 ounces frozen berries, thawed and drained
- Thin strips of lemon zest for garnish

TO MAKE THE CREMA: In a food processor, combine all of the ingredients and process until smooth and creamy, 2 to 3 minutes. Transfer to a bowl and refrigerate until well chilled, about 1 hour.

In a small saucepan over medium-high heat, bring the Chambord to a simmer. Adjust the heat to maintain a simmer and continue to cook until reduced by half to form a syrup, about 10 minutes. Refrigerate until well chilled.

When the crema and syrup are cold, divide the crema among four dessert bowls or small glasses, or, for a fittingly elegant presentation, spoon the crema into a beautiful glass bowl. Spoon the berries and Chambord syrup over the crema. Garnish with a strip of lemon zest before serving.

Orange and Saffron Paletas

Paletas, which is Spanish for "ice pops," have a long history in Mexico, where they come in every flavor imaginable. They're perfect in the summer—not only because they're a great way to cool off, but because they take full advantage of summer's bounty of fruit. Orange and saffron are a detour from more traditional Mexican flavors, putting a Middle Eastern spin on this south-of-the-border treat. This recipe specifies using ice pop molds, but if you don't have them, it's easy to improvise; for example, you could use paper cups and wooden craft sticks.

MAKES 10 PALETAS; SERVES 10

¼ **cup sugar**

¾ **cup water**

¼ **teaspoon saffron threads**

2 **oranges, peeled and separated into segments**

2 **cups fresh orange juice**

1 **teaspoon orange flower water**

In a small saucepan, combine the sugar and water. Bring to a boil over medium-high heat, stirring occasionally. Continue boiling and stirring until the sugar dissolves. Remove from the heat, stir in the saffron, and set aside until cool.

If the oranges have seeds, remove them, then put the segments in a blender. Add the saffron syrup, orange juice, and orange flower water and blend until smooth.

Divide the mixture evenly among ten 2½-ounce molds, insert the sticks, and freeze until solid, 3 to 4 hours. To serve, dip the bottom of the molds in warm water for 3 to 4 seconds, then remove the covers and pull out the paletas.

Ginger Pound Cake

WITH MATCHA GLAZE

Any vegan baker has to find a good substitute for those pesky eggs and dairy products so commonly used in baked goods, and pound cake, traditionally made with a pound each of butter, eggs, flour, and sugar presents a special challenge. Thanks to my baking guru, Christine Moore, this delicious vegan pound cake overcomes all obstacles. It is as close in taste and texture to a conventional pound cake as possible for a vegan version. While there are a multitude of flavor additions that might elevate this humble dessert to the hedonistic plane, I think the pairing of crystallized ginger and matcha, a fine powder made from the highest-quality Japanese green tea leaves, does it beautifully.

YIELD 1 LOAF; SERVES 8 TO 10

CAKE

- 1 cup cold vegan shortening, diced, plus more for greasing the pan
- 1 cup sugar
- 2 teaspoons pure vanilla extract
- 14 ounces unsweetened plain soy yogurt
- 2½ cups all-purpose flour
- 2 teaspoons baking powder
- 1 teaspoon baking soda
- ½ teaspoon salt
- ½ cup coarsely chopped crystallized ginger

MATCHA GLAZE

- 1 cup powdered sugar
- 4 teaspoons matcha
- 2 tablespoons water

TO MAKE THE CAKE: Preheat the oven to 350°F. Grease a 9-by-5-inch loaf pan, with shortening. In the bowl of a stand mixer fitted with the paddle attachment, combine the shortening and sugar and beat on medium speed until light and fluffy, about 3 minutes, scraping down the sides of the bowl halfway through. Add the vanilla and continue beating for 1 minute. Turn the mixer speed to low, add the yogurt, and continue beating until combined.

CONTINUED

Sift the flour, baking powder, baking soda, and salt into a separate bowl. Add one-third of the flour to the yogurt mixture and mix at low speed with quick, short, on-and-off intervals, occasionally scraping down the sides of the bowl with a spatula, until combined. Repeat twice more to incorporate all of the dry ingredients.

Pour the batter into the prepared pan and smooth the top with the back of a wet spoon. Sprinkle the crystallized ginger over the top, then bake for 45 to 55 minutes, until a cake tester, bamboo skewer, or toothpick inserted in the middle of the cake comes out clean. Let the cake cool in the pan on a wire rack for 20 minutes.

MEANWHILE, MAKE THE GLAZE: In a small bowl, combine the powdered sugar, matcha, and water and whisk until thoroughly combined.

Remove the cake from the pan, put it on the rack, and let cool completely before drizzling the glaze over the top. Transfer to a serving platter, slice, and serve.

Pistachio Olive Oil Cake

I developed this dessert with the help of a good friend and recipe goddess, Christine Moore, owner of Little Flower Candy Co. in Pasadena, California. This rich cake is topped off with a compote that's packed with a fruit basket's worth of flavor, made from a whole orange and lemon, peel and all, and enhanced with Grand Marnier. To add to the visual appeal, a scattering of jewel-like red pomegranate seeds rests as a final garnish.

MAKES ONE 9-INCH CAKE; SERVES 8 TO 10

CAKE

- ⅓ cup extra-virgin olive oil, plus more for greasing the pan
- ⅔ cup shelled pistachios (3 ounces), toasted (see Tip, page 101)
- ½ cup plain unsweetened soy yogurt
- 6 ounces soft silken tofu
- ¾ cup sugar
- 1 teaspoon pure vanilla extract
- 1 cup all-purpose flour
- ½ teaspoon baking powder
- ½ teaspoon baking soda
- ¼ teaspoon salt

TOPPING

- 1 orange
- 1 lemon
- 1 cup water
- ½ cup sugar
- ¼ cup Grand Marnier or other orange liqueur

- ¼ cup shelled pistachios (1¼ ounces), toasted (see Tip, page 101) and coarsely chopped
- ¼ cup fresh pomegranate seeds

CONTINUED

TO MAKE THE CAKE: Preheat the oven to 325°F. Oil the bottom and sides of a 9-inch cake pan, then line with a piece of parchment paper cut to fit the bottom of the pan and oil the parchment paper (or use baking spray with flour).

In a food processor, pulse the pistachios until finely ground. But don't overdo it, or they'll turn into nut butter.

In the bowl of a stand mixer fitted with the paddle attachment, combine the yogurt, tofu, sugar, olive oil, and vanilla and beat at medium speed until well combined.

Sift the flour, baking powder, baking soda, and salt into a separate bowl. Add to the tofu mixture and beat until well combined. Add the ground pistachios and beat again until incorporated.

Pour the batter into the prepared cake pan and bake for 25 to 30 minutes, until a cake tester, bamboo skewer, or toothpick inserted in the middle of the cake comes out clean. Let the cake cool briefly, then invert onto a wire rack, remove the pan, and let cool completely.

TO MAKE THE TOPPING: Slice the orange and lemon in half, then cut into ¼-inch slices. Remove the seeds. In a medium saucepan, combine the orange, lemon, water, sugar, and Grand Marnier. Bring to a boil over high heat, stirring occasionally, then lower the heat, cover, and simmer until the fruit is soft and pliable and starting to break down, about 1 hour.

Transfer the mixture to a food processor and pulse repeatedly until thick and chunky.

Spread the topping evenly over the top of the cake. Garnish with chopped pistachios and pomegranate seeds before serving.

CHAPTER 3

Evening

Blood Orange Margarita

This blood-red version of the classic frozen margarita features agave syrup (obtained from the same species of agave plant used to make tequila) and manifests an orange-flavored double threat with the blood orange juice and Grand Marnier. Look for blood oranges from late fall to early spring. You can also purchase blood orange juice online year-round.

{ **SERVES** 4 }

3 **cups crushed ice (see Tip)**

12 **ounces blood orange juice, preferably fresh**

Juice of 1 lime

6 **ounces 100% agave tequila**

2 **ounces Grand Marnier or other orange-flavored liqueur**

2 **ounces agave syrup**

Blood orange slices for garnish

Chill four margarita or old-fashioned glasses in the freezer for at least 10 minutes.

In a blender, combine the ice, orange juice, lime juice, tequila, Grand Marnier, and agave syrup and blend on high speed until smooth and slushy. Serve in the chilled glasses with a blood orange slice on each rim as garnish.

TIP: If you don't have crushed ice, don't fret; you can still have frozen margaritas. Simply put some ice in a heavy canvas sack or wrap it in a clean kitchen towel and pound it with a rolling pin, a hammer, or the bottom of a heavy skillet. In a pinch you can use whole ice cubes, but the consistency of the finished drink might not be as smooth. Another alternative is to serve the margaritas up. Put the orange juice, lime juice, tequila, Grand Marnier, and agave syrup in a blender and blend until thoroughly combined, then pour into four glasses filled with ice cubes.

Mexican White Russian

This multicultural take on a White Russian is much more complex than the heavy drink of your college days. It makes use of horchata, a traditional Latin American beverage typically made with rice and almonds. Its thirst-quenching properties provide the perfect foil to any dish with hot chiles. You can substitute store-bought horchata, but I recommend that you make it from scratch; I guarantee that it will taste better than anything that's been sitting on the shelf for a month. One important note: The horchata isn't labor-intensive to make, but it is a lengthy process, so making this cocktail does require that you plan ahead.

{ **SERVES 1** }

Ice cubes

1 ounce vodka

4 ounces horchata (page 118)

1 ounce Kahlúa or other coffee liqueur

Cinnamon stick for garnish

Fill a cocktail shaker with ice. Add the vodka, horchata, and Kahlúa and shake well. Fill an 8-ounce old-fashioned glass or lowball tumbler with ice. Strain the cocktail into the glass and add the dual-purpose cinnamon stick, which serves as both garnish and swizzle stick. Serve immediately.

Horchata

{ MAKES 6 CUPS }

- ½ **cup white jasmine rice**
- ½ **cup blanched raw almonds (2 ounces)**
- One **3- to 4-inch cinnamon stick, broken into a few pieces**
- 2 **cups hot water**
- 1 **cup sugar**
- 4 **cups cold water**
- ½ **teaspoon pure vanilla extract**

In a heatproof bowl or pitcher, combine the rice, almonds, cinnamon, and hot water. Cover and let steep at room temperature for at least 6 hours and up to overnight.

In a medium saucepan, combine the sugar and cold water. Bring to a boil over medium-high heat, stirring occasionally, and continue boiling and stirring until the sugar dissolves. Set aside to cool.

Transfer the rice mixture to a blender, including the cinnamon, and process until smooth, about 3 minutes. Line a colander with three layers of dampened cheesecloth, then put the colander over a larger bowl. Strain the blended mixture into the bowl; be patient and give it time to seep through. Don't press the solids to extract the maximum amount of liquid, or the horchata will have sediment in it. Discard the solids. Stir the sugar syrup into the strained mixture and stir. Add the vanilla and stir once more. Refrigerate the horchata for at least 1 hour, until well chilled. Store in an airtight container in the refrigerator for up to 4 days. Stir the horchata well before each use.

Garbanzo Bean Socca

A regional specialty native to the city of Nice in the south of France, *socca* is a thin, pizzalike flatbread made from garbanzo bean flour and olive oil. The French have been known to get a little cranky when anyone outside of Provence attempts to make *socca*, but I don't see why we can't all give it a try. That said, don't even think of serving it with any wine other than a Provençal rosé. Use raw garbanzo bean flour if you can find it. Otherwise, the toasted variety is fine.

························{ **SERVES 6** }························

1¼ **cups garbanzo bean flour**

1 **teaspoon salt**

1 **teaspoon chopped fresh thyme**

1 **cup water**

6 **tablespoons extra-virgin olive oil**

1 **teaspoon chopped fresh rosemary**

Freshly ground pepper

Smoked Spanish or plain paprika for dusting

In a medium bowl, combine the garbanzo bean flour, salt, thyme, water, and 2 tablespoons of the olive oil and whisk vigorously until there are no lumps. Let the batter rest for 20 minutes to 1 hour.

Position an oven rack 4 to 5 inches from the broiler and put a 12-inch ovenproof skillet in the oven. Preheat the oven to 450°F.

Once the oven has preheated, take out the hot skillet and coat it with 2 tablespoons olive oil, swirling to evenly coat the inside surface. Whisk the batter once again, then pour all of it into the prepared skillet. Drizzle the top with the remaining 2 tablespoons olive oil. Bake for 6 to 8 minutes, until the edges begin to develop a blistered crust. Turn on the broiler, put the skillet in the oven, and cook just until the top begins to brown, 2 to 3 minutes.

Sprinkle the rosemary over the top, then dust with the pepper and paprika. Cut into wedges and serve warm.

PARCHMENT
Flatbread Crackers

These ultrathin crackers are only masquerading as a flatbread. They're essentially made by baking pasta dough, and in fact, if you own a pasta machine, you can use it to roll out the dough (see Tip). Sprinkled with salt and aromatic fresh rosemary, these crackers are a crisp, rustic snack, and as beautiful to look at as they are delicious.

{ **MAKES 8; SERVES 4 TO 6** }

1 **cup semolina, plus more for dusting**

1 **cup all-purpose flour, plus more for dusting**

¾ **teaspoon salt, plus more for sprinkling**

¾ **cup warm water**

2 **tablespoons extra-virgin olive oil, or as needed**

1 **tablespoon coarsely chopped fresh rosemary**

1½ **tablespoons kosher or Maldon sea salt**

In a large bowl, combine the semolina, flour, and salt and stir until well mixed. Slowly add the water, stirring continuously with a wooden spoon until thoroughly combined. Using your hands, gather the dough and form it into a ball.

Transfer the dough to a lightly floured work surface and knead until firm and smooth but not sticky, 2 to 3 minutes. Cover with plastic wrap and let rest for 30 minutes.

Preheat the oven to 450°F and put a pizza stone or an inverted baking sheet in the oven.

Divide the dough into eight portions, shape them into balls, and cover with a towel or plastic wrap. Working with one piece of dough at a time and keeping the rest covered, flatten the ball into a disk with the palm of your hand. Dust your work surface and rolling pin liberally with flour and roll the disk into as thin a round as possible. Keep moving and turning the dough as you roll to prevent it from sticking, dusting your rolling pin and work surface with more flour as needed. You may end up with a shape that's more oblong than round;

either is fine. The goal is to achieve a rustic shape that's rolled out as thin as possible. Prick dough with the tines of a fork every few inches.

Using a semolina-dusted pizza peel or inverted baking sheet, transfer one or two sheets of dough to the pizza stone or baking sheet in the oven. Bake for 2 minutes, then remove from the oven with tongs and place on a clean work surface, inverting so the side that was touching the pizza stone now faces up. Brush the top lightly with olive oil and sprinkle with about ⅜ teaspoon of the rosemary and ½ teaspoon of the salt. Return to the oven, oiled-side up and bake for 2 minutes, until golden brown. Keep a close eye on the cracker, as it can burn quickly. Transfer to a wire rack to cool for 5 to 10 minutes.

Repeat with the remaining dough. Store in an airtight container at room temperature for up to 1 day.

TIP: If you own a pasta machine, you can use it to roll out the dough. Once you've shaped the dough into eight balls, flatten one piece into a disk, then dust it very lightly with flour using a dry pastry brush or sprinkling just a bit of flour on by hand. Set the pasta machine at the widest setting (usually number 1) and feed the disk of dough through. Fold the resulting sheet in half and feed through at the same setting once more to give it an extra kneading. Set the machine one setting thinner, dust the dough with more flour, and pass it through the machine one time. Continue in this way, each time at the next-thinner setting, until the dough is thin and almost translucent. It could be as much as a few feet long; if larger than your pizza stone or baking sheet, cut it in half crosswise to fit. Prick with the tines of a fork every few inches and bake as directed.

(No) Cheese Plate

Let's cut to the chase: cheese isn't the only food that can accentuate the subtle flavor of wine. My (No) Cheese Plate pays tribute to those foods that often accompany the fromage, which I have always found much more interesting anyway. I've included fig paste in the shape of coins, deep red quince paste (otherwise known as *membrillo* in Spain), and thin, sweet pear chips, all prepared in unusual ways intended to bring out the unique flavors of these fruits. To assemble the (No) Cheese Plate, arrange pieces of the fig paste, quince paste, and pear chips in small clusters. Add some fresh fruit, a hearty loaf of bread, and a few Spiced Nuts (page 180), then pour yourself a glass of crisp Viognier and put on a little Edith Piaf. *Je ne regrette rien . . .*

{ **SERVES 4 TO 6** }

Fig Paste

- 1 **teaspoon fennel seeds**
- ¼ **cup hazelnuts, toasted and skinned (see Tip, page 203)**
- 1¼ **cups stemmed, halved dried black Mission figs**
- 1 **tablespoon brandy**
- 1½ **teaspoons balsamic vinegar**
- 1½ **teaspoons water**
- ⅛ **teaspoon freshly ground pepper**

Preheat the oven to 200°F.

In a small skillet, toast the fennel seeds over medium heat just until they start to change color. Transfer to a spice mill or clean coffee grinder and grind into a powder. In a food processor, combine the hazelnuts, figs, brandy, vinegar, and water and process to form a paste. Add the ground fennel and pepper and pulse until evenly incorporated.

Transfer the fig paste to a sheet of aluminum foil. Shape it into a rough 6-inch log, then wrap it tightly in the foil and roll to shape it into a cylinder. Unwrap the foil and put the log, still on the foil, on a baking sheet. Bake for 20 to 25 minutes, until the surface of the log dries and hardens a bit. Cool the log completely before wrapping it securely in clean foil. Store in an airtight container in the refrigerator for up to 2 months. Serve sliced into coins, cold or at room temperature.

CONTINUED

Quince Paste

2 pounds ripe, fragrant quinces
2 to 3 teaspoons canola oil
2 to 3 cups sugar
1 tablespoon fresh lemon juice
Fresh bay leaves (optional)
4 cups water

Wash the quinces to remove any fuzz on the skin. Peel and core the quinces, but don't discard the peels and cores. In a deep saucepan, combine the peels and cores, and add water to cover (about 4 cups). Bring to a boil over medium-high heat, then continue to boil, stirring occasionally, for 30 minutes. Strain and return the liquid to the saucepan. Discard the peels and cores.

Slice the quinces, add them to the saucepan, and bring to a simmer over medium-high heat. Lower the heat and simmer for 1 hour, stirring occasionally. Line a fine-mesh sieve with three layers of cheesecloth, then pour in the quince mixture. Let most of the liquid drain out, then gather the cheesecloth and tie with string to secure the bundle. Hang the bundle in the refrigerator with a container underneath to catch the liquid and let drain for at least 12 hours.

Generously coat a rimmed baking sheet with the canola oil.

Using a food mill or food processor, finely grind the quince flesh. Measure the quince purée, then put it in a wide, heavy pot with an equal amount of sugar. Add ¼ cup of water for each 1 cup of quince purée. Cook over medium-low heat, stirring occasionally, until the sugar dissolves. Add the lemon juice. Bring to a boil, then lower the heat and simmer, stirring frequently to prevent scorching, for about 45 minutes, until the paste pulls away from the sides of the pot and the color is dark orange. Before the paste cools, quickly pour it on the prepared baking sheet and spread it out to a thickness of ¾ inch. Cover the top with cheesecloth and set aside in a cool place for 4 days.

Cut into 3-inch squares and stack with fresh bay leaves (if using) or parchment paper between the layers. Store in an airtight container in the refrigerator for up to 1 month.

Pear Chips

2 slightly underripe pears
¾ cup sugar

Preheat the oven to 200°F. Line a rimmed baking sheet with a silicone baking mat or parchment paper.

Using a mandoline or very sharp knife, cut the pears lengthwise into very thin slices; don't remove the seeds or cores. Put the sugar on a plate, then dip the pears slices in the sugar, turning to coat both sides. Transfer to the prepared baking sheet, arranging them in a single layer.

Bake for about 1 hour, until the edges of the pears begin to curl. Turn the slices over and bake for another 1 hour or so, until golden brown. Transfer the pears to a wire rack. Cool before serving.

Grilled Tofu Grape Leaves

Technically, these are stuffed grape leaves, but they aren't really dolmas, those traditional Middle Eastern appetizers usually stuffed with rice. In this version, tofu is marinated in a Provençal mixture of olive oil, oregano, thyme, mint, and garlic. Then it's bundled up into tidy grape-leaf packages tied with kitchen twine and grilled. Be sure to store unopened jars of grape leaves in a cool, dark place so the leaves keep their color.

··{ **SERVES 6 TO 8** }··

36 grape leaves packed in brine

1 cup fresh lemon juice

2 cups extra-virgin olive oil

¼ cup coarsely chopped fresh oregano

¼ cup chopped fresh thyme

¼ cup coarsely chopped fresh mint

8 garlic cloves

1 teaspoon salt

½ teaspoon freshly ground pepper

1¾ pounds extra-firm tofu, drained and cut crosswise into eighteen ½-inch slices

Fill a large saucepan with water and bring to a boil over high heat. Put the grape leaves in the boiling water, remove from the heat, and let soak for 20 minutes. Drain, then fill the pot with fresh, cold water. Drain and repeat, filling the pot with cold water and draining once again. Spread the leaves on a few clean kitchen towels to dry a bit.

In a medium bowl, combine the lemon juice, olive oil, oregano, thyme, mint, garlic, salt, and pepper and whisk until thoroughly combined. Add the tofu slices and marinate for at least 1 hour and up to overnight, turning once.

CONTINUED

On a clean work surface, arrange two grape leaves, one slightly overlapping the other. Place a slice of the marinated tofu in the center, then fold the leaves over to completely encase the tofu like a package. Secure with kitchen twine. Put the packet in a large, shallow baking pan, then repeat with the remaining grape leaves and tofu. Pour the remaining marinade over the packets.

Prepare a medium-hot outdoor grill or heat a grill pan on the stovetop over medium-high heat. Grill the packets until the grape leaves are browned and crispy but not falling apart, about 2 minutes per side. Transfer to a platter and serve right away.

Yuba Spring Rolls

Most Westerners aren't familiar with yuba, but I have a feeling that's about to change. A traditional food from China and Japan, yuba is the skin that forms on the surface of heated soymilk. It's gently lifted off the simmering soymilk in sheets and either used fresh or dried and then reconstituted. It has a slightly nutty flavor and a chewy texture. Yuba is available at most well-stocked Asian markets; however, if it proves difficult to find, packaged egg roll wrappers make an acceptable substitute.

MAKES 12 ROLLS; SERVES 6 AS AN APPETIZER

3 tablespoons peanut oil, plus more for frying

10 ounces shiitake mushrooms, stemmed and sliced

6 ounces extra-firm tofu, drained

4 green onions (white and green parts), thinly sliced

One 2-inch piece fresh ginger, peeled and cut into thin matchsticks

4 garlic cloves, minced

3 tablespoons soy sauce

3 tablespoons toasted sesame oil

3 tablespoons mirin or Chinese sweet cooking wine

1 tablespoon tapioca starch

1½ teaspoons water

12 sheets fresh or dried yuba or 6-inch square egg roll wrappers

In a medium skillet, heat 2 tablespoons of the peanut oil over medium-high heat. Add the mushrooms and sauté until softened, 3 to 5 minutes. Transfer to a large bowl (no need to clean the skillet).

Pat the tofu lightly with a paper towel or clean kitchen towel to remove excess moisture, then cut it into ½-inch dice. In the same skillet, heat the remaining 1 tablespoon of peanut oil over medium heat. Add the green onions, ginger, and tofu and sauté for 2 to 3 minutes. Add the garlic and sauté for 30 seconds. Transfer to the bowl along with mushrooms.

In a small bowl, combine the soy sauce, sesame oil, and mirin and stir until well mixed. Pour 3 tablespoons of the mixture over the mushrooms and tofu and stir gently to combine. Reserve the remaining soy sauce mixture to use as a dipping sauce.

CONTINUED

In a small bowl, combine the tapioca starch and water and mix to form a paste.

If using dried yuba, soak the sheets in cold water for 5 minutes, then drain and stack between slightly damp kitchen towels.

Trim the sheets of yuba to 6-inch squares. On a clean work surface, place one sheet in front of you at a diagonal. Place 2 to 3 tablespoons of the tofu mixture on the corner closest to you. Lifting the corner point, gently fold the yuba and filling over toward the center of the sheet. Fold the left and right corners toward the center to enclose the filling on the sides. Then continue rolling away from you until you reach the top corner. Secure the roll by dipping a finger in the bowl of tapioca starch and using it to paste the top corner of the yuba sheet to the roll. Repeat with the remaining sheets.

In a large, heavy skillet, heat 1 inch of peanut oil over medium-high heat. Fry the rolls until golden brown, about 1 minute on each side. Transfer to paper towels or a wire cooling rack to drain. Stir the reserved soy sauce mixture well, then serve it alongside the yuba rolls as a dipping sauce.

Tomato and Three-Bean Salad

This salad, with its combination of fresh green beans, roasted cherry tomatoes, and two varieties of cooked beans has enough color and texture to keep all of your senses busy. Using canned beans is a convenience, but if you're feeling ambitious, go the extra mile and cook up some dried beans to use instead. You could also get creative and swap out other varieties of beans for the kidney and butter beans and the salad will be just as delicious.

······························{ **SERVES 4 TO 6** }······························

1 **pint cherry tomatoes**

1½ **teaspoons salt**

1 **pound fresh green beans, trimmed**

1 **tablespoon extra-virgin olive oil**

4 **shallots, thinly sliced**

One **15-ounce can red kidney beans, drained**

One **15-ounce can butter beans, drained**

1 **cup coarsely chopped fresh parsley**

⅓ **cup Wendy's Vinaigrette (page 86)**

Freshly ground pepper

1 **lemon, cut into wedges**

Preheat the oven to 375°F.

For cherry tomatoes less than ½ inch in diameter, leave them whole; cut larger ones in half. Put the tomatoes on a rimmed baking sheet cut-side up and sprinkle with 1 teaspoon of the salt. Bake for 40 minutes, until the tops begin to slightly char. Set aside to cool.

Meanwhile, prepare an ice-water bath by filling a large bowl with ice and water.

Bring a large pot of water to a boil. Add the green beans and cook until tender, 5 to 8 minutes. Drain, then immediately plunge the beans into the ice-water bath to stop the cooking process and set the beautiful green color of the beans. When cooled, drain the beans and spread them on a clean kitchen towel to dry

CONTINUED

In a small skillet, heat the olive oil over medium-low heat. Add the shallots and sauté until they begin to caramelize, 5 to 6 minutes. Season with the remaining ½ teaspoon salt and remove from the heat.

In a large mixing bowl or salad bowl, combine the green beans, kidney beans, butter beans, and parsley, then add the shallots and tomatoes, including any juices in their pans. Stir gently to combine, then drizzle the vinaigrette over everything. Toss gently until everything is evenly coated. Season with pepper, then taste and adjust the seasoning if you like. Squeeze the lemon wedges over the salad just before serving.

Moroccan Orange Salad

Like an oasis in the desert, this perfumed salad combines an exotic array of ingredients with sweet, juicy oranges. Pomegranate molasses (a sweet-tart syrupy reduction of pure pomegranate juice), three varieties of orange flavor, nuts, and dried fruit are interwoven to create a tapestry of color and scents.

{ **SERVES 6** }

12 oranges

⅓ cup pomegranate molasses

⅓ cup agave syrup

¼ cup Grand Marnier or other orange liqueur

2 teaspoons orange blossom water

12 dates, pitted and chopped

⅓ cup shelled pistachios, toasted (see Tip, page 101) and chopped

3 tablespoons chopped fresh mint

Working over a large bowl to catch the juice, use a sharp paring knife to trim the peel and white pith away from the oranges. Remove the seeds and cut into 1-inch dice, or simply separate the sections.

In a small bowl, combine the pomegranate molasses, agave syrup, Grand Marnier, and orange blossom water and stir until smooth.

In a large serving bowl, combine the oranges, dates, and pistachios and stir gently until well combined.

To serve the salad chilled, refrigerate the orange mixture for 1 to 2 hours, or you can serve it right away at room temperature. In either case, just before serving, pour the pomegranate molasses mixture over the salad, stir gently until everything is evenly coated, then garnish with the mint.

Brussels Sprout Slaw

If you have memories of being forced to eat Brussels sprouts boiled, overcooked, and soggy, don't hold that against this diminutive cruciferous vegetable. The Brussels sprouts in this dish are served raw, preserving their formidable nutritional profile and allowing their flavor to sing. If anyone at your table falls into the anti–Brussels sprouts contingency, they should be pleasantly disarmed when they realize what they're eating.

{ **SERVES 6** }

2 pounds Brussels sprouts

1 cup walnuts (4 ounces), toasted (see Tip, page 101) and coarsely chopped

¼ cup nutritional yeast flakes

2 tablespoons extra-virgin olive oil

2 tablespoons fresh lemon juice

1 teaspoon salt

½ teaspoon freshly ground pepper

Wash the Brussels sprouts and discard any discolored outer leaves. Trim away the base and gently separate the layers of leaves. Transfer the leaves to a bowl. Add the walnuts, nutritional yeast, olive oil, and lemon juice. Toss until everything is well combined. Season with the salt and pepper and toss once more. Serve immediately.

Lapsang Souchong Rice

Lapsang souchong is a smoked black tea from China. Here I use it to impart its distinct aroma and taste to rice. Depending on how much smokiness you want, you can steep the rice in the tea briefly or really give it time to soak in. If you're a real fan of the flavor, you can even leave the tea leaves in the rice while it cooks. This rice is a nice accompaniment for Broiled Tofu, Carrots, and Shiitake Mushrooms (page 99).

{ **SERVES** 4 }

2½ **tablespoons Lapsang souchong tea leaves**

2 **cups boiling water**

1½ **cups white jasmine rice**

1 **teaspoon salt**

In a heatproof bowl or teapot, combine the tea and boiling water. Cover and let steep for 5 minutes. Strain through a fine-mesh sieve set over a medium saucepan and let cool.

In a large bowl, rinse the rice with cold water until the water runs clear. Drain and add to the tea. Stir in the salt and let sit for 30 minutes.

Put the saucepan over medium-high heat and bring to a boil. Lower the heat, cover, and simmer until the liquid has been absorbed and the rice is tender, 15 to 20 minutes. Let stand for 5 minutes before serving.

Nutty Mushroom Risotto

Making risotto need not be so daunting. It truly isn't complex. The only thing you need to make great risotto is patience; you cannot cut corners or multitask while preparing this dish. If you want that creamy consistency characteristic of authentic risotto, you must stir the dish constantly during cooking, adding the stock slowly and repeatedly as directed.

{ **SERVES 4** }

6 cups vegetable stock, preferably homemade (see page 98)

4 tablespoons extra-virgin olive oil

10 ounces mixed wild mushrooms (such as oyster, chanterelle, or stemmed shiitake) thinly sliced

2 teaspoons chopped fresh thyme, plus 4 sprigs fresh thyme for garnish

¾ cup finely chopped shallots

1 cup Arborio rice

½ cup dry white wine

½ cup hazelnuts (2 ounces), toasted and skinned (see Tip, page 203) and coarsely chopped

Salt

Freshly ground pepper

In a medium saucepan, bring the stock to a simmer over medium heat. Adjust the heat to maintain a simmer as you prepare the rice and mushrooms.

In a large saucepan, heat 1 tablespoon of the olive oil over medium heat. Add the mushrooms and sauté until softened, 2 to 3 minutes. Add the thyme and sauté for 1 minute. Transfer to a bowl.

Add the remaining 3 tablespoons olive oil to the saucepan, still over medium heat. Add the shallots and sauté until translucent, 2 minutes. Add the rice and cook, stirring constantly, for 3 to 4 minutes. Add the wine and continue to cook, stirring constantly, until almost all of the wine has been absorbed by the rice.

CONTINUED

Add a ladleful of the simmering stock to the rice and continue to cook, stirring constantly, until almost all of the stock has been absorbed. Add another ladleful of stock and continue cooking in the same way, stirring continuously and adding more stock each time the rice has absorbed almost all of the previous addition. This entire process will take about 15 to 20 minutes; in the end, the rice should be rich and creamy but still al dente, firm with some resistance.

Add the mushrooms and hazelnuts and stir gently to combine. Remove from the heat and season with salt and pepper. Serve immediately in warmed bowls, garnished with the thyme sprigs.

Polenta

WITH WILD MUSHROOMS, HAZELNUTS, AND FIGS

Wild mushrooms, hazelnuts, figs, and thyme all make me think of the Pacific Northwest, so I came up with this dish to showcase the earthy flavors of an Oregon forest. The black currant dressing makes for a snazzy presentation that's guaranteed to impress. While the preparation may seem a bit elaborate, this dish is well worth the effort. And if you like, you can prepare the polenta and lentils in advance.

································{ SERVES 4 }································

FIGS

- 4 dried black Mission figs, stemmed
- 1 cup black currant juice or 100% pomegranate juice

BLACK CURRANT DRESSING

- Reserved black currant juice (from the figs)
- 1½ teaspoons Dijon mustard
- Juice of ½ lime
- 2 teaspoons minced shallot
- 1 tablespoon crème de cassis
- 1 tablespoon red wine
- 2 tablespoons balsamic vinegar
- ½ cup hazelnut oil
- Salt
- Freshly ground pepper

- 3 tablespoons extra-virgin olive oil, plus more for oiling the pan and brushing
- 9 cups water
- Salt
- 2 cups polenta
- 1 cup French green lentils, rinsed and drained
- Freshly ground pepper
- 2 tablespoons chopped shallot
- 10 ounces mixed wild mushrooms (such as oyster, chanterelle, and stemmed shiitake), thinly sliced
- 2 tablespoons hazelnuts, toasted and skinned (see Tip, page 203) and finely chopped
- 1 teaspoon chopped fresh thyme
- Baby lettuce, arugula, or micro-greens for garnish

CONTINUED

TO PREPARE THE FIGS: Put the figs in a small bowl. In a small saucepan, bring the black currant juice to a boil over high heat. Pour the juice over the figs and let stand for 30 minutes. Drain, reserving the juice, and coarsely chop the figs.

TO MAKE THE DRESSING: In a small saucepan, heat the reserved black currant juice over medium heat. Cook, stirring occasionally, until reduced to about 2 tablespoons, 20 to 30 minutes. Transfer the reduction to a blender. Add the mustard, lime juice, shallot, crème de cassis, wine, and vinegar and blend until smooth. With the motor running, slowly drizzle in the hazelnut oil and blend until the mixture is thick and smooth. Season with salt and pepper, then transfer to a squeeze bottle or bowl.

Lightly coat a 9-inch square baking pan with olive oil. In a large saucepan, combine 6 cups of the water and salt over high heat. Bring to a boil over medium-high heat, then slowly add the polenta, whisking constantly and vigorously to break up any lumps. Lower the heat to maintain a gentle boil and cook, stirring occasionally, until very thick and pulling away from the sides of the pan, about 20 minutes. Pour the polenta into the prepared pan and use the back of a wet spoon or a wet spatula to spread it in an even, flat layer and smooth the surface. Cover with plastic wrap and refrigerate until firm, at least 15 minutes.

Put the lentils in a medium saucepan and add the remaining 3 cups water. Cover and bring to a boil over high heat, then lower the heat and simmer until soft, 30 to 45 minutes. Drain, then season with salt and pepper.

In a large skillet, heat the 3 tablespoons olive oil over medium-high heat. Add the shallot and mushrooms and sauté until softened, 2 to 3 minutes. Add the figs, hazelnuts, and thyme and sauté for 3 to 4 minutes.

Preheat a medium-hot outdoor grill or heat a grill pan on the stovetop over medium-high heat. Cut four 3-inch circles of polenta using a biscuit cutter, glass, or, in a pinch, a large can with the top and bottom removed. (Save the scraps for another use.) Brush olive oil on both sides of the polenta and grill until the bottom is browned and the polenta no longer sticks to the grill, about 5 minutes. Turn and grill the other side until browned, about 5 minutes.

Reheat the lentils and mushrooms if need be. Spoon one-fourth of the lentils in a 4-inch pool in the center of each plate. Place a polenta round on top of the lentils. Spoon one-fourth of the mushroom mixture over the polenta, then top with a few leaves of the baby lettuce. Drizzle 2 to 3 tablespoons of the dressing over the top and around each plate and serve immediately, with the remaining dressing alongside.

Celery Root and Fennel Chowder

Rich and creamy as any New England–style chowder, this verdant soup blends celery root and sweet fennel with chunky potatoes in a vegetable-only version. The word *chowder* is a corruption of the French *chaud*, or "hot," but to me chowder just means throwing a bunch of ingredients that go well together into a pot, *voilà tout*. For the perfect chowdery texture, be sure to dice or mince the vegetables precisely. However, in the spirit of an unfussy Maine fisherman, don't worry too much about the proportions—just resist the urge to throw in some oyster crackers.

SERVES 4 TO 6

1 large fennel bulb, trimmed and thinly sliced, plus 2 tablespoons of fennel fronds reserved for garnish

2 to 3 leeks, white part only, well cleaned and thinly sliced

2 large potatoes, peeled and cut into ½-inch dice

1 or 2 shallots, minced

3 garlic cloves, minced

1 cup minced fresh parsley

1 teaspoon minced fresh thyme

2 teaspoons fennel seeds

2 teaspoons salt

½ teaspoon freshly ground pepper

¼ teaspoon red pepper flakes

¼ cup extra-virgin olive oil

1 large celery root, peeled and cut into ½-inch dice

6 cups water

In a deep soup pot, combine the sliced fennel, leeks, potatoes, shallots, garlic, parsley, thyme, fennel seeds, salt, pepper, and red pepper flakes. Drizzle the olive oil over the top, then stir well until the vegetables are evenly coated. Put the pot over medium-low heat, cover, and simmer for 15 to 20 minutes, stirring a few times to keep the vegetables from sticking to the bottom of the pot.

Stir in the celery root and water. Raise the heat to medium-high and bring to a boil. Continue to cook at a boil, stirring occasionally, until the celery root is tender, about 20 minutes.

Transfer half of the mixture to a blender and process until smooth. Pour the purée back into the soup pot and stir until well mixed. Taste and adjust the seasonings if you like. Serve in warmed soup bowls garnished with the fennel fronds.

CONFUSED
Artichoke Soup

Pity the poor, confused Jerusalem artichoke. It's not from Jerusalem, and it's not related to the artichoke. It's also known as the sunchoke, since it's actually the root of a plant in the sunflower family. I personally like the name Jerusalem artichoke, as it lends an air of the exotic. As a gesture toward resolving this tuber's long-standing identity crisis, I came up with this recipe to showcase its fine qualities, then developed the variation to highlight the distinct differences between the Jerusalem artichoke and the equally delicious true artichoke. The homemade aioli drizzle is a nice touch, but if you don't have the time or inclination to make it, you can substitute Vegenaise, made by Follow Your Heart, with a few pressed garlic cloves mixed in.

SERVES 4

2 tablespoons extra-virgin olive oil

1 large yellow onion, chopped

3 garlic cloves, peeled and coarsely chopped

1½ pounds Jerusalem artichokes, peeled and cut into 1-inch dice

5 cups vegetable stock, preferably homemade (see page 98)

½ teaspoon salt

1 or 2 grinds of black pepper

4 tablespoons Vegan Aioli (page 150) for drizzling

In a large saucepan, heat the olive oil over medium-high heat. Add the onion and sauté until soft and translucent, about 5 minutes. Add the garlic and sauté for 30 seconds. Add the Jerusalem artichokes, stock, salt, and pepper and bring to a boil. Lower the heat, cover, and simmer until the vegetables are tender, 10 to 15 minutes.

In a blender, blend the soup in small batches until smooth. Return the purée to the pan and stir well. Taste and add more salt and pepper if you like. Ladle into warmed soup bowls and drizzle 1 tablespoon of the aioli over each before serving.

VARIATION:
Artichoke Heart Soup

Substitute 1 pound of thawed frozen artichoke hearts for the Jerusalem artichokes.

Vegan Aioli

[**MAKES ¾ CUP**]

4 ounces soft silken tofu
1 tablespoon vinegar (rice or cider)
½ teaspoon Dijon mustard
1 tablespoon sugar
¼ teaspoon salt
2 garlic cloves, minced
½ teaspoon lemon zest
3 threads saffron
2 tablepoons canola oil
2 tablepoons olive oil

In a food processor or blender, combine the tofu, vinegar, mustard, sugar, salt, garlic, lemon zest and saffron and process until smooth. With the machine running, drizzle in the canola oil and olive oil in a thin, slow stream and continue processing until the aioli is smooth and emulsified. The aioli will keep, refrigerated and covered, for up to 3 days.

Roasted Brown Bag Vegetables

This rustic dish pairs roasted vegetables (three root vegetables and one thistle) with a homemade aioli. Each vegetable is combined with a complementary herb and roasted slowly en papillote, in this case in its own private paper bag. This is a fun dish for a dinner party, with the bags pulling double duty, transforming into unique serving containers at the table.

-------------------------------{ SERVES 6 }-------------------------------

ARTICHOKES

Juice of 1 lemon

2 pounds baby artichokes

1 tablespoon extra-virgin olive oil

4 sprigs fresh thyme

½ teaspoon salt

¼ teaspoon freshly ground pepper

POTATOES

12 ounces Russian fingerling potatoes

1 tablespoon extra-virgin olive oil

8 garlic cloves, unpeeled, smashed

4 small sprigs fresh rosemary

1 teaspoon salt

½ teaspoon freshly ground pepper

CARROTS

8 ounces baby carrots, trimmed to 2 inches, or large carrots cut into 2-inch pieces

1 tablespoon extra-virgin olive oil

1 tablespoon chopped fresh parsley

½ teaspoon salt

¼ teaspoon freshly ground pepper

ONIONS

12 ounces pearl onions, preferably a mix of red, white, and yellow

1 tablespoon extra-virgin olive oil

8 garlic cloves, unpeeled, smashed

1 tablespoon coarsely chopped fresh sage

½ teaspoon salt

½ teaspoon freshly ground pepper

¾ cup Vegan Aioli (page 150) for serving

CONTINUED

Preheat the oven to 400°F.

TO PREPARE THE ARTICHOKES: Fill a large bowl with water and add the lemon juice. Trim the dark, tough outer leaves from the artichokes, stopping when you reach the tender, yellowish green inner leaves. Using a small, sharp knife, cut off the top ½ inch of each artichoke. Trim the stems and all remaining dark green areas from the base. As you finish trimming each artichoke, put it in the lemon water to prevent discoloring. You should end up with about 1 pound of trimmed artichokes.

Drain the artichokes, then dry them with a clean kitchen towel. In a large bowl, combine the artichokes, olive oil, thyme, salt, and pepper. Toss until the artichokes are evenly coated, then transfer to a clean brown paper lunch bag. Fold down the top couple of inches of the bag, then invert the bag, fold-side down, on a baking sheet.

TO PREPARE THE POTATOES: Clean the potatoes, using a scrub brush if necessary to remove any dirt. Leave their skins on. In the same bowl used for the artichokes, combine the potatoes, olive oil, garlic, rosemary, salt, and pepper. Toss until the potatoes are evenly coated, then transfer to a clean brown paper lunch bag. Fold down the top couple of inches of the bag, then put it, fold-side down, on the baking sheet next to the artichokes.

TO PREPARE THE CARROTS: Clean the carrots with a scrub brush. If carrots are longer than the width of the paper bag, trim them down to fit. In the same bowl, combine the carrots, olive oil, parsley, salt, and pepper. Toss until the carrots are evenly coated, then transfer to a clean brown paper lunch bag. Fold down the top couple of inches of the bag, then put it, fold-side down, on the baking sheet next to the potatoes.

TO PREPARE THE ONIONS: Leave the skins on the onions. In the same bowl, combine the onions, olive oil, garlic, sage, salt, and pepper. Toss until the onions are evenly coated, then transfer to a clean brown paper lunch bag. Fold down the top couple of inches of the bag, then put it, fold-side down, on the baking sheet next to the carrots.

Put the baking sheet with the four bags of vegetables in the oven and roast for 1 hour. Let cool until you can handle the paper comfortably. Invert each bag, placing it right-side up, and open the bag completely. Roll down the top of each bag until the vegetables are exposed, being careful not to tear the paper, which may have become brittle in the oven.

Serve the bags on a tray or platter, with the aioli alongside in a bowl for dipping and let everyone help themselves. Provide a small empty bowl for the garlic and onions skins.

Potato Torte

Potato and *torte* are two of my favorite words, not to mention two of my favorite foods, so I thought, "Why not put them together?" The thin slices of potato are coated with a savory mixture of olive oil, garlic, and rosemary. Tapioca starch and lecithin help bind the layers together, but you can omit them if you prefer a flakier texture. The springform pan helps give the dish its height, making for an impressive presentation. Plus, unlike a standard baking pan, it's easy to remove after baking. Don't fight with your tablemates for the crispy crust on top; there will be plenty to go around.

{ SERVES 8 }

¾ cup extra-virgin olive oil, plus more for oiling the pan

2 tablespoons tapioca starch

2 tablespoons unsweetened plain soymilk

2 tablespoons liquid lecithin

3 garlic cloves, minced

2 teaspoons salt

1 teaspoon coarsely ground pepper

2 teaspoons minced fresh rosemary

4 pounds Yukon gold or other baking potatoes, unpeeled

3 teaspoons nutritional yeast flakes, or as needed

Preheat the oven to 400°F. Coat a 9-inch springform pan with olive oil and put it on a rimmed baking sheet.

In a small bowl, combine the tapioca starch and soymilk and stir to form a thick paste. In a large bowl, combine the olive oil, lecithin, garlic, salt, pepper, rosemary, and tapioca mixture and whisk until well combined.

Clean the potatoes, using a scrub brush if necessary to remove any dirt, then dry them with a clean kitchen towel. Using a mandoline or a sharp knife, cut the potatoes lengthwise into ⅛-inch slices. Add them to the olive oil mixture and toss gently until evenly coated.

CONTINUED

Layer one-fourth of the potato slices in the bottom of the prepared springform pan, overlapping each piece slightly on top of the previous to form a circular fan shape. Sprinkle 1 teaspoon of the nutritional yeast over the potatoes. Continue layering the potatoes and sprinkling the yeast, ending with a final layer of potatoes. Drizzle any remaining oil from the bowl over the top. Oil a sheet of parchment paper or foil, then place it on top of the torte, oiled-side down. Press down on the parchment paper to compress the potato layers as much as possible.

Bake for 1 hour, then remove the parchment paper and bake for 30 minutes, until a skewer easily pierces all the way through the torte.

Let cool to room temperature. Carefully loosen the pan and separate the torte from the pan with a spatula. Cut into wedges and serve.

Poblano Chiles Rellenos

Poblano chiles are a mild, medium to large pepper all too often mislabeled "pasillas" in supermarkets. Here they're filled with a savory mixture of fresh corn and zucchini. The crema will blow your mind, as the cashews are transformed into a silky-smooth cream with the most incredible flavor. A slightly acidic tomatillo-cilantro sauce provides the perfect complementary final touch.

SERVES 4

4 poblano chiles

TOMATILLO SALSA

8 ounces tomatillos, husked and rinsed

4 shallots, unpeeled

4 garlic cloves, unpeeled

1 bay leaf

1 tablespoon extra-virgin olive oil

2 tablespoons fresh lime juice

2 teaspoons tequila

¼ cup minced fresh cilantro

½ teaspoon sea salt

1 tablespoon extra-virgin olive oil

1¼ cups corn kernels (from about 2 ears of corn)

½ medium red onion, diced

1 cup chopped zucchini, cut into ¼-inch dice

½ teaspoon sea salt

¼ teaspoon freshly ground pepper

1 tablespoon minced fresh flat-leaf parsley

2 tablespoons minced fresh chives

1 recipe Cashew Crema (page 53)

Cilantro sprigs for garnish

CONTINUED

Preheat the oven to 400°F.

Roast the poblanos over a medium to high gas flame on either the stovetop or an outdoor grill. Use tongs to turn the peppers repeatedly until most of the skin is charred, blackened, and slightly blistered. Be careful not to overcook the peppers, or they may split and be difficult to peel. Put them in a heat-proof bowl and cover with a plate or plastic wrap to allow them to steam.

When the roasted peppers are cool enough to handle, gently peel away the skin using your fingers or a small paring knife. Resist the urge to run the peppers under water, as this will remove their nice smoky flavor. Make a slit down one side of each pepper below the stem. Leave the stem intact and remove the seeds.

TO MAKE THE SALSA: In a large bowl, combine the tomatillos, shallots, garlic, bay leaf and olive oil. Spread the mixture on a rimmed baking sheet and bake for 12 to 15 minutes, until the tomatillos are slightly charred and have released some of their juices. Remove from the oven and lower the oven temperature to 375°F.

When cool enough to handle, remove and discard the bay leaf and the skins from the shallots and garlic. Transfer the tomatillos, shallots, garlic, and any pan juices to a blender. Add the lime juice, tequila, cilantro, and salt and blend until smooth.

Spoon half of the salsa into a 9-by-13-inch baking pan and spread to evenly cover the bottom.

In a medium saucepan, heat the olive oil over medium heat. Add the corn, onion, and zucchini and sauté until the onion is translucent, 5 to 8 minutes. Stir in the salt and pepper, then transfer to a large, clean bowl.

Stir the parsley and chives into the crema, then add the crema to the corn mixture and stir gently until well mixed.

Stuff each pepper with one-fourth of the corn mixture (about ½ cup). Arrange the peppers in the baking pan on top of the salsa. Bake for 25 minutes, until heated through. Spoon the remaining salsa over the peppers. Garnish with the cilantro sprigs, and serve right away.

Eggplant Parma-Style

Parma, a city in the Italian region of Emilia-Romagna, is well-known for its architecture and, of course, its cuisine. This recipe incorporates some of the best that cuisine has to offer. For optimum flavor, make this dish in summer, with the freshest local eggplant and basil, just as the inhabitants of Parma would. That way you can also make the sauce from scratch using fresh, whole tomatoes. Still, you may want to make this hearty dish in winter, in which case canned tomatoes are probably your best bet, so that's what the recipe actually calls for. I suggest you splurge and use not just any canned tomatoes, but canned tomatoes from San Marzano, Italy. These flavorful plum tomatoes are grown in the volcanic soil beneath Mount Vesuvius. Though nowhere near Parma, they are so special they have their own DOC (*denominazione di origine controllata*), a seal that stipulates they can only come from San Marzano. Read labels closely and don't be fooled by imitations that use tomatoes grown in the United States.

{ **SERVES 4 TO 6** }

2 tablespoons extra-virgin olive oil, plus more for oiling the pan and frying

½ medium yellow onion, minced

2 garlic cloves, minced

One 28-ounce can crushed or diced tomatoes, preferably San Marzano (to use fresh tomatoes, see Tip)

2 large eggplants

Salt

Freshly ground pepper

1 teaspoon dried oregano, or 1 tablespoon minced fresh oregano

2 tablespoons minced fresh flat-leaf parsley

1 recipe Cashew Crema (page 53)

1 bunch fresh basil, stemmed and leaves torn into large pieces

3 tablespoons dried bread crumbs

Preheat the oven to 400°F. Coat an 8-inch square baking pan with olive oil.

In a large skillet, heat the 2 tablespoons olive oil over medium-low heat. Add the onion and sauté until soft and translucent, about 5 minutes. Add the garlic and sauté for 30 seconds. Add the tomatoes and their juices and cook, stirring occasionally until thick, 25 to 30 minutes. Let cool, then transfer to a blender or food processor and blend until smooth.

Trim the ends of the eggplants, then cut the eggplants lengthwise into ¼-inch-thick slices. In a large skillet, heat ¼ inch of olive oil over medium-high heat. Put as many eggplant slices as will fit in the skillet and cook until golden brown, turning once, 2 to 3 minutes per side. Transfer to paper towels to drain, then season lightly with salt and pepper. Repeat with the remaining eggplant.

Stir the oregano and 1 tablespoon of the parsley into the crema.

Spread one-fourth of the tomato sauce (about ½ cup) on the bottom of the prepared pan, then arrange one-third of the eggplant slices on top of the sauce. Sprinkle one-third of the basil leaves over the eggplant slices. Spread one-third of the crema (about ½ cup) evenly over the basil leaves. Repeat the layers two more times: sauce, eggplant, basil, and crema. Spread the remaining sauce over the last layer of crema, then sprinkle the bread crumbs over the top.

Bake for 45 to 60 minutes, until the top is beginning to brown and the juices are bubbling. Let stand for 15 minutes to set up before cutting and serving.

TIP: To make the sauce using fresh, peak-of-season tomatoes, bring a large pot of water to a boil and, working in batches, blanch 4 to 5 pounds of tomatoes until their skins split and blister (30 to 40 seconds). Using a slotted spoon, transfer the tomatoes to an ice bath. When cool enough to handle, peel the skins away, halve the tomatoes, and scoop out and discard the seeds. Coarsely chop the tomatoes and use them in place of the canned tomatoes in the recipe.

Zucchini Lasagna

WITH PESTO

In this unconventional lasagna, blanched leek and ribbons of roasted zucchini stand in for the noodles, and a thick pine nut crema replaces the ricotta. But in a nod to tradition, it's smothered in a sauce made from San Marzano tomatoes, along with a garlicky basil pesto. Like so many casseroles, this lasagna is even better the next day . . . if there's any left, that is. One note: The preparation time is lengthy (though most of it isn't hands-on time). Read through the recipe thoroughly and plan accordingly.

{ SERVES 6 }

VEGETABLES

- 4 large tomatoes, preferably heirloom, cut crosswise ¼ inch thick
- 4 medium zucchini, cut lengthwise ¼ inch thick
- 1 teaspoon extra-virgin olive oil
- Salt
- 1 large leek, at least 2 inches in diameter

PINE NUT CREMA

- 1 cup raw pine nuts (4 ounces)
- 1 cup raw cashew pieces (5 ounces)
- 2 tablespoons fresh lemon juice
- 1 tablespoon extra-virgin olive oil
- 1 tablespoon nutritional yeast flakes
- ½ cup water
- ½ teaspoon sea salt
- ¼ teaspoon freshly ground pepper

TOMATO SAUCE

- 2 tablespoons extra-virgin olive oil
- ½ medium yellow onion, chopped
- One 28-ounce can crushed tomatoes, preferably San Marzano (to use fresh tomatoes, see Tip, page 161)
- One 6-ounce can tomato paste
- 1 teaspoon dried oregano
- 1 teaspoon salt
- ½ teaspoon freshly ground pepper
- Pinch of red pepper flakes

PESTO

- 3 garlic cloves
- ½ cup walnuts (2 ounces), toasted (see Tip, page 101)
- 2 cups packed fresh basil leaves
- ¼ teaspoon salt
- ½ teaspoon freshly ground pepper
- ½ cup extra-virgin olive oil

- Extra-virgin olive oil for oiling the pan
- ¾ cup dried bread crumbs
- Fresh basil leaves for garnish

TO PREPARE THE VEGETABLES: Preheat the oven to 350°F. Arrange the tomatoes and zucchini in a single layer on a rimmed baking sheet, keeping them separate. Drizzle with the olive oil, sprinkle lightly with salt, and bake for 1 hour, until the tomatoes have lost most of their moisture.

Meanwhile, trim away the dark green parts and root end of the leek. Carefully cut lengthwise halfway through the leek. Separate the layers and rinse thoroughly to remove any grit. Fill a medium saucepan with water and bring to a boil over high heat. Add the leek strips and blanch for just 10 to 15 seconds, then drain immediately.

AS THE TOMATO AND ZUCCHINI CONTINUE TO BAKE, MAKE THE CREMA: In a food processor, combine all of the ingredients and process until smooth and creamy, 2 to 3 minutes.

AS THE VEGETABLES CONTINUE TO BAKE, MAKE THE TOMATO SAUCE: In a medium saucepan, heat the olive oil over medium heat and sauté the onion until translucent, about 5 minutes. Stir in the crushed tomatoes, tomato paste, oregano, salt, pepper, and red pepper flakes. Lower the heat and simmer, stirring occasionally, until thickened, about 15 minutes.

MEANWHILE, MAKE THE PESTO: With the food processor running, drop the garlic in through the feed tube and process until the garlic is minced, about 10 seconds. Turn the processor off, add the remaining pesto ingredients, and process until smooth.

Raise the oven temperature to 375°F. Coat a 9-by-13-inch baking pan or casserole with olive oil.

Line the bottom of the baking pan with a layer of zucchini slices. Spread 1 cup of the tomato sauce over the zucchini, then top with half of the leeks in an even layer. Spread half of the crema evenly over the leeks, then top with half of the roasted tomatoes in an even layer. Sprinkle ¼ cup of the bread crumbs over the tomatoes. Top with the remaining leeks, then spread all of the pesto evenly over the leeks. Top with the remaining roasted tomatoes. Sprinkle another ¼ cup of bread crumbs over the tomatoes, then spread the remaining crema over the top. Spread the remaining tomato sauce over the crema and, finally, top with the remaining ¼ cup of bread crumbs.

Bake for 45 to 50 minutes, until the top is browned and the juices are bubbling. Let stand for 10 minutes to set up before cutting. Garnish with the fresh basil leaves and serve right away.

Seared Tofu

WITH DATE BARBECUE SAUCE

I should have called this Date Barbecue Sauce with Seared Tofu because the sauce is really the star. Nonetheless, the ever-versatile tofu provides a strong supporting role as a blank backdrop against which to enjoy the dramatically spicy sauce, thickened with sticky-sweet dates.

.................................{ **SERVES 4** }.................................

BARBECUE SAUCE

- ¼ teaspoon saffron threads
- 1 tablespoon water
- ¼ cup extra-virgin olive oil
- 1 medium yellow onion, finely chopped
- 1 tablespoon ground coriander
- 1 teaspoon ground cumin
- 1 teaspoon smoked Spanish paprika
- 1 teaspoon ground ginger
- 1 teaspoon ground cinnamon
- 1 teaspoon salt
- ½ teaspoon freshly ground pepper
- 4 garlic cloves, minced
- ¼ cup tomato paste
- 3 cups vegetable stock, preferably homemade (see page 98)
- 2 tablespoons brown sugar
- ½ teaspoon cayenne pepper
- 10 large dates, pitted and minced
- ¼ cup fresh lemon juice

- 1¾ pounds extra-firm tofu, drained and pressed (see Tip)
  Canola oil, for greasing the pan

TO MAKE THE BARBECUE SAUCE: In a small bowl, combine the saffron and water and let sit for at least 10 minutes. In a medium saucepan, heat the olive oil over medium-low heat. Add the onion and sauté until soft and translucent, 8 to 10 minutes. Stir in the coriander, cumin, paprika, ginger, cinnamon, salt, and pepper and continue to cook, stirring occasionally, for 5 minutes. Add the garlic and sauté for 30 seconds. Add the tomato paste, stock, brown sugar, cayenne, and saffron water to the onion mixture, turn the heat to medium-high and cook, stirring often, until the sauce begins to thicken, 8 to 10 minutes. Add the dates, lower the heat, and simmer, stirring occasionally, until thick and fragrant, about 15 minutes. Remove from the heat and stir in the lemon juice.

CONTINUED

Preheat the oven to 250°F. Cut the tofu into thick slices. Lightly oil a large grill pan or heavy skillet with the canola oil and put it over medium-high heat. Dredge half of the tofu slices in the barbecue sauce, then put them in the pan and cook until browned on the bottom, about 5 minutes; if using a grill pan, you should begin to see nice grill marks forming. Turn and cook until browned on the other side, about 5 minutes. Transfer the tofu to a serving platter and put it in the oven to keep warm. Apply additional oil to the pan as needed and cook the remaining tofu in the same way. Serve the tofu with the remaining barbecue sauce alongside.

TIP: To press tofu, wrap each block in a clean kitchen towel, then put the tofu on a rimmed baking sheet. Put a second baking sheet on top of the tofu and set a weight (such as a heavy skillet, a large jug of water, or even a brick) on top, centering the weight over the tofu and being careful not to use so much weight that you squash the tofu, rather than simply pressing the water out. Press for at least 20 minutes.

Blueberry and Earl Grey Sorbet

I love the sexy, midnight-blue color of this dessert. Blueberries are infused with Earl Grey, a black tea blended with oil from the rind of bergamot (a fragrant variety of citrus), then puréed and frozen. The two flavors seem to intertwine, like a young couple in love.

{ **MAKES 1 QUART; SERVES 4 TO 6** }

½ **cup sugar**

½ **cup water**

1 **tablespoon Earl Grey tea leaves**

¼ **teaspoon salt**

5 **cups fresh or frozen, thawed blueberries**

2 **tablespoons fresh lemon juice**

In a small saucepan, combine the sugar, water, and tea leaves. Bring to a boil over medium-high heat, stirring occasionally. Stir in the salt, lower the heat, and simmer for 2 minutes. Transfer the syrup to a bowl and let cool to room temperature. Strain the syrup, discarding the tea leaves.

In a blender, combine the syrup, blueberries, and lemon juice and blend until smooth. Strain the purée through a fine-mesh sieve, pressing with a spatula to extract as much liquid as possible. Discard the seeds and skin. Cover and refrigerate for at least 1 hour and up to overnight.

Freeze in an ice-cream maker according to the manufacturer's instructions. Transfer to a freezer-safe container, cover, and freeze until firm, about 1 hour.

Espresso Gelato

Traditional gelato has less air churned into its base than ice cream and is therefore denser. This nondairy version has just the right creamy texture and smooth mouthfeel. Be sure to chill the base thoroughly before pouring it into the ice-cream maker in order to prevent ice crystals from forming. You may have noticed that I like presenting flavor options in sets of three, so here they are: Espresso Gelato has bits of whole espresso beans stirred in at the end; Mexican Chocolate Gelato is made with authentic vanilla-laced Ibarra chocolate; and Piñon Gelato is made with toasted pine nuts.

MAKES 1 QUART; SERVES 4 TO 6

2 tablespoons tapioca starch

3 cups unsweetened plain soymilk

¾ cup sugar

2 tablespoons liquid lecithin

1 tablespoon canola oil

⅛ teaspoon salt

1 teaspoon pure vanilla extract

¼ cup freshly brewed espresso or strong coffee

1 teaspoon coarsely chopped espresso-roast coffee beans

In a small bowl, combine the tapioca starch and ¼ cup of the soymilk and mix to form a paste. In a medium saucepan, combine the remaining 2¾ cups soymilk with the sugar, lecithin, canola oil, and salt. Bring to a boil over medium heat, stirring occasionally. Add the tapioca mixture, lower the heat, and simmer until the mixture thickens slightly, about 2 minutes.

Remove from the heat, stir in the vanilla and espresso, then strain through a fine-mesh sieve. Stir in the espresso beans and refrigerate for at least 3 hours or preferably overnight.

Freeze in an ice-cream machine according to the manufacturer's directions. Transfer to a freezer-safe container, cover, and freeze until firm, at least 2 hours. Shortly before serving, remove from the freezer and let stand at room temperature for 10 minutes to soften slightly.

CONTINUED

VARIATION:
Mexican Chocolate Gelato

Prepare as directed, omitting the espresso and espresso beans. When simmering the soymilk mixture, add 2 disks of Ibarra Mexican chocolate (about 6 ounces), coarsely chopped, and stir until melted.

VARIATION:
Piñon Gelato

Toast ¾ cup (3 ounces) of pine nuts (see Tip, page 101), then coarsely chop them. Prepare as directed, omitting the espresso and espresso beans. When simmering the soymilk mixture, add the chopped pine nuts. When straining the gelato base, press the solids with a spatula to extract as much liquid as possible.

Basmati Rice Pudding

If you've read through even just a few of the recipes in this book, it should be fairly obvious that I have a fetish for exotic spices. Most of us think of rice pudding as a bland cafeteria dish, but this take on *kheer*, the traditional rice pudding popular in India, is anything but. Teaming up one of my favorite flavor trifectas—saffron, cardamom, and pistachio—with the perfumed scent of rose water, this recipe elevates rice pudding to delectable heights.

························{ **SERVES 4** }························

2 **tablespoons tapioca starch**

5 **cups rice milk**

½ **cup white basmati rice**

6 **cardamom pods**

⅓ **cup sugar**

¼ **teaspoon rose water**

Pinch of saffron threads

Pinch of salt

2 **tablespoons shelled pistachios, toasted (see Tip, page 101) and coarsely chopped**

In a small bowl, combine the tapioca starch and ¼ cup of the rice milk and mix to form a paste. Set aside for 10 minutes.

In a large saucepan, combine the remaining 4¾ cups rice milk with the rice, cardamom, sugar, and tapioca mixture. Bring to a boil over medium-high heat, stirring frequently. Lower the heat to maintain a high simmer and cook, stirring occasionally, until the mixture has reduced by about two-thirds, about 30 minutes.

Fish out and discard the cardamom pods. Add the rose water, saffron, salt, and 1 tablespoon of the pistachios and stir briefly to combine. Transfer to a bowl, cover with plastic wrap, and refrigerate until well chilled, at least 1 hour.

To serve, spoon the pudding into four individual bowls and garnish with the remaining pistachios.

CHAPTER 4

Late
Night

Rosewater Hot Chocolate

Nothing tastes better than a cup of hot chocolate on a cold night, but this version raises the bar. Saffron and chile de árbol spike this drink, lending it a touch of earthiness and bit of heat. But the star attraction is rose water, which, when blended with the chocolate, transforms this childhood staple into an elixir worthy of Scheherazade.

{ **SERVES 4** }

4 **cups unsweetened plain soymilk**

1 **teaspoon rose water**

½ **teaspoon saffron threads, lightly crushed**

2 **sticks cinnamon**

1 **chile de árbol**

½ **vanilla bean, split lengthwise, or 1 teaspoon pure vanilla extract**

¼ **cup sugar**

4 **ounces bittersweet chocolate, coarsely chopped**

In a medium saucepan, combine the soymilk, rose water, saffron, cinnamon, chile, vanilla, and sugar over medium heat. Cook, stirring occasionally until the mixture begins to steam and almost comes to a boil. Lower the heat and simmer for 10 minutes. Remove from the heat and let steep for 15 minutes more.

Strain, discarding the spices, and return the soymilk to the pot. Add the chocolate, put the pot over medium-low heat, and cook, whisking briskly, until the chocolate is entirely melted, about 5 minutes. Serve in warmed mugs.

Lemon Verbena Bellini

As classy as a formal black-tie event, this drink takes its cue from the classic peach cocktail invented at Harry's Bar in Venice, Italy. Once you've made the syrup, simply put it out in a pitcher with a couple of chilled bottles of bubbly and let guests make their own drinks. The frozen lemonade concentrate used to make the syrup is infused with lemon verbena, rendering it intoxicatingly fragrant.

------------------------------{ **SERVES 8** }------------------------------

One   **12-ounce can frozen lemonade concentrate, thawed**

½   **cup fresh lemon verbena leaves**

Two   **750-ml bottles sparkling wine (champagne, Prosecco, or cava), chilled**

In a medium saucepan, combine the lemonade concentrate and lemon verbena over medium-low heat. Simmer, stirring occasionally, until slightly reduced, syrupy, and fragrant, 10 to 15 minutes. Strain, discarding the lemon verbena, and cool to room temperature.

For each cocktail, pour 2 tablespoons of the syrup into a champagne flute, then slowly fill the glass with sparkling wine. Serve immediately.

Lavender-Tangerine Martini

Preparing this cocktail is like bartending in a citrus orchard. The combination of the floral scent of lavender and the bright, fresh taste of tangerines is positively Mediterranean. The gorgeous color of tangerine juice is also a welcome change from the usual palette of pinkish Cosmopolitans and greenish Appletinis.

{ **SERVES 1** }

Ice cubes

2 ounces vodka

½ ounce Grand Marnier or other orange liqueur

2 ounces fresh tangerine juice

1 ounce lavender simple syrup (recipe follows)

½ ounce fresh lemon juice

Fresh lavender sprigs or a twist of tangerine peel for garnish

Chill a martini glass in the freezer for at least 10 minutes.

Fill a cocktail shaker with ice, then add the vodka, Grand Marnier, tangerine juice, simple syrup, and lemon juice. Shake vigorously until well chilled, about 10 seconds. Strain into the chilled glass and garnish with the lavender sprigs.

Lavender Simple Syrup

[MAKES 1 CUP]

½ cup sugar

½ cup water

1½ tablespoons dried or fresh lavender flowers

In a small saucepan, combine the sugar and water. Bring to a boil over medium-high heat, stirring until the sugar dissolves. Remove from the heat, add the lavender, and let steep for 30 minutes. Strain and store in an airtight container in the refrigerator for up to 1 month.

Curried Chickpea Snack

Crunchy, salty, spicy—in other words, plays well with cocktails. I'm totally addicted to these lightly fried snacks and can't keep myself from reaching for the bowl. If you're like me, you'll find that this recipe only makes enough for yourself, so you might want to double or even triple the recipe if you have to share.

MAKES 2 CUPS; SERVES 1 TO 4

Two 15-ounce cans garbanzo beans
2 teaspoons curry powder
2 teaspoons chili powder
½ cup all-purpose flour
Canola oil for frying
Salt
Smoked Spanish paprika

Drain and rinse the garbanzo beans, then put them on a clean kitchen towel and pat dry.

In a large bowl, combine the garbanzo beans, curry powder, and chili powder and toss until evenly coated. Add the flour and toss again until evenly coated.

In a large frying pan, heat ¼ inch of oil to 365°F. Add the garbanzo beans in small batches and fry until browned and crispy, 6 to 8 minutes. Drain on paper towels and season with salt and paprika. Serve warm.

Spiced Nuts

This collection of recipes goes all out, with six different types of toasted nuts: almonds, cashews, peanuts, pistachios, walnuts, and pepitas. True, pepitas, being pumpkin seeds, aren't technically a nut, but they fill the same niche. This is irresistible party food and, needless to say, the perfect match to any cocktail. Prepare one, some, or all of them, according to your preferences or whims.

....{ **MAKES 2 CUPS EACH** }..

Maple-Ginger Almonds

¼ **cup soy sauce**

¼ **cup maple syrup**

1 **tablespoon extra-virgin olive oil**

1 **teaspoon ground ginger**

2 **cups raw almonds (9 ounces)**

Preheat the oven to 350°F.

In a medium bowl, combine the soy sauce, maple syrup, olive oil, and ginger and stir until well mixed. Add the almonds and toss until evenly coated.

Spread the almonds in an even layer on a rimmed baking sheet and bake for about 15 minutes, until deep brown, stirring once about halfway through. Transfer to a clean baking sheet and let cool, tossing frequently to prevent sticking. Transfer to a serving bowl.

Smoky Cashews

1 **dried chipotle mora chile, or**
  ½ **teaspoon ground chiles**

2 **cups raw whole cashews**
  (9 ounces)

1 **teaspoon smoked Spanish paprika**

1 **tablespoon extra-virgin olive oil**

2 **teaspoons salt**

Use a spice mill to finely grind the chile. In a dry, heavy skillet, toast the cashews over medium heat, shaking frequently, until fragrant, about 10 minutes. Transfer to a bowl; add the ground chile, paprika, olive oil, and salt; and toss until evenly coated. Transfer to a serving bowl.

Chile Peanuts

1 tablespoon fresh lime juice

1 tablespoon extra-virgin olive oil

1 teaspoon smoked Spanish paprika

2 teaspoons salt

½ teaspoon New Mexico chile powder

2 cups unsalted dry-roasted peanuts (9 ounces)

Preheat the oven to 250°F.

In a medium bowl, combine the lime juice, olive oil, paprika, salt, and chile powder and stir until well mixed. Add the peanuts and toss until evenly coated. Spread the peanuts in an even layer on a rimmed baking sheet and bake for about 30 minutes, until golden brown, stirring once halfway through. Transfer to a serving bowl.

....

Vanilla-Mint Pistachios

2 cups shelled raw pistachios (9 ounces)

1 tablespoon extra-virgin olive oil

1 teaspoon pure vanilla extract

1 tablespoon finely chopped fresh mint

1 teaspoon salt

Preheat the oven to 350°F.

Spread the pistachios in a single layer on a rimmed baking sheet, and bake for 7 to 8 minutes, until lightly toasted and fragrant.

In a medium bowl, combine the olive oil, vanilla, mint, and salt and stir until well mixed. Add the pistachios and toss until evenly coated. Put the pistachios back on the baking sheet, spread them in an even layer, and bake for about 15 minutes, until golden brown, stirring once about halfway through. Transfer to a serving bowl.

CONTINUED

Curried Walnuts

2 cups raw walnut halves (9 ounces)
1 tablespoon toasted sesame oil
1 teaspoon curry powder
1 tablespoon sesame seeds
½ teaspoon salt

Preheat the oven to 350°F.

In a medium bowl, combine the walnuts and sesame oil and toss until evenly coated.

Spread the walnuts in an even layer on a rimmed baking sheet, and bake for 7 to 8 minutes, until lightly toasted and fragrant.

In a clean medium bowl, combine the curry powder, sesame seeds, and salt and stir until well mixed. Add the walnuts and toss until evenly coated. Put the walnuts back on the baking sheet and bake for 5 minutes. Transfer to a serving bowl.

Spicy Pepitas

1 tablespoon extra-virgin olive oil
2 cups raw pepitas (8 ounces)
2 teaspoons sugar
1 teaspoon salt
½ teaspoon ground cumin
½ teaspoon New Mexico chile powder
¼ teaspoon ground cinnamon

In a heavy skillet, heat the olive oil over medium heat. Add the pepitas and cook, stirring frequently, until they are evenly toasted and begin to pop, about 5 minutes. Stir in the sugar, salt, cumin, chile powder, and cinnamon and cook, stirring constantly, for 1 minute. Transfer to a serving bowl.

Vegan Tapas Plate

We're having a tapas party! Traditionally, tapas were small plates of food set down, free of charge, for customers at Spanish bars and restaurants. Unfortunately, as their popularity increased, so did the price. These three recipes make for a nicely rounded tapas plate. And after you've made these a few times, you should feel confident and inspired to improvise and expand your repertoire. I recommend serving a nice Albariño or Tempranillo wine as an accompaniment.

······································{ **SERVES 4 TO 6** }································

Potatoes with Aioli

2 tablespoons extra-virgin olive oil

1 teaspoon salt

1 teaspoon smoked Spanish paprika

4 medium potatoes, unpeeled and cut into 1-inch dice

½ cup Vegan Aioli (page 150) for dipping

Preheat the oven to 450°F.

In a large bowl, combine the olive oil, salt, and paprika and stir until well mixed. Add the potatoes and toss until evenly coated. Spread the potatoes on a rimmed baking sheet and bake for 20 to 30 minutes, until browned and slightly crispy.

Transfer the potatoes to a platter and serve with the aioli alongside in a small bowl, with toothpicks to facilitate dipping.

CONTINUED

Warm Olives and Almonds

2 cups assorted olives, such as picholine, kalamata, and niçoise

1 cup raw almonds (4½ ounces)

1 cup extra-virgin olive oil

½ cup garlic cloves, peeled

3 sprigs fresh thyme

In a large sauté pan over medium heat, combine all of the ingredients and cook, stirring occasionally, until the almonds begin to brown and the garlic is tender, about 15 minutes. Discard the thyme. Using a slotted spoon, transfer the olives, almonds, and garlic to a serving bowl. Serve warm, with toothpicks alongside.

Garlic Mushrooms

½ cup extra-virgin olive oil

2 pounds small cremini or button mushrooms, stems trimmed

½ cup dry white wine

3 sprigs fresh thyme

3 sprigs fresh oregano

2 bay leaves

6 garlic cloves, sliced

Grated zest and juice of 2 lemons

Salt

Freshly ground pepper

In a large skillet, heat ¼ cup of the olive oil over medium heat. Add the mushrooms, wine, thyme, oregano, and bay leaves. Cook, stirring occasionally, until the wine has evaporated, about 3 minutes. Add the garlic and sauté for 30 seconds. Remove from the heat and stir in the lemon zest and juice and the remaining olive oil. Season with salt and pepper. Pour into a serving bowl and let cool. Serve at room temperature, with toothpicks alongside.

Vanilla Coconut Flan

I don't recall the moment when flan was elevated from its humble vanilla-infused caramel custard roots to it current gourmet status, but I'm definitely on board. For this vegan version, a coconut-milk base is gelled with agar, a flavorless substance derived from seaweed, creating a wonderfully soft final texture. In addition to the fairly standard vanilla version, I've included two tasty variations: ginger and green tea.

················{ **SERVES 6** }················

½ **cup sugar**

2¼ **cups coconut milk**

1 **tablespoon agar flakes, or 1 teaspoon agar powder**

6 **ounces soft silken tofu**

2 **tablespoons agave syrup**

1 **teaspoon pure vanilla extract**

Pinch of salt

Unsweetened shredded coconut, toasted (see Tip, page 101), for garnish

Put the sugar in a small saucepan over medium-low heat and cook, stirring, until the sugar is melted and caramelized. Pour it into six 5-ounce ramekins or custard molds, dividing it evenly among them. Swirl the ramekins to evenly coat the bottoms with the caramelized sugar.

Put the coconut milk in a medium saucepan and sprinkle with the agar. Let sit for 10 to 20 minutes to soften the agar. Bring to a boil over high heat, then lower the heat and simmer, stirring often, until the agar has dissolved, about 5 minutes.

In a blender, combine the coconut milk mixture, tofu, agave syrup, vanilla, and salt and purée until smooth. Pour the mixture into the ramekins, then cover with plastic wrap. Refrigerate until chilled and firm, about 2 hours.

To serve, briefly dip the bottom of each ramekin in hot water, just for 15 seconds or so. Remove the plastic wrap and invert the ramekin onto a plate, pouring any remaining caramel over the flan. Garnish the top of each with a sprinkling of coconut.

Ginger Flan

Prepare as directed, omitting the vanilla extract and adding 1 tablespoon of grated peeled fresh ginger or 1 teaspoon of ground ginger. After inverting onto serving plates, garnish the tops with chopped crystallized ginger rather than the coconut.

Green Tea Flan

Prepare as directed, omitting the vanilla extract and adding 1 tablespoon of matcha powder. After inverting onto serving plates, garnish the tops with whole green tea leaves rather than the coconut.

Tea-Poached Pears
IN CARAMEL SAUCE

In this recipe, twin pear preparations combine for an elegant dessert. Fresh pears are poached in a flowery sugar syrup infused with jasmine tea, then they're topped with a sophisticated caramel sauce based on pear juice. It's not as daunting as you might think, but I suggest you read through the recipe closely before you begin cooking, and that you remove all sources of distraction when preparing the sauce.

{ SERVES 4 }

SAUCE

- 2 cups pear juice, bottled or freshly juiced
- 1 cup sugar
- ¼ cup water

POACHED PEARS

- 4 ripe pears
- ¼ cup fresh lemon juice
- 3 cups cold water
- 3 tablespoons jasmine tea leaves
- ½ cup sugar

TO MAKE THE SAUCE: Put the pear juice in a medium saucepan over medium heat and cook, stirring occasionally, until reduced to ½ cup, about 40 minutes. Set aside to cool.

In medium saucepan, combine the sugar and water. Stir just until combined; it should have the consistency of a thick paste. Slowly bring the mixture to a boil, without stirring, over medium heat. Resist the urge to stir or do anything other than use a damp pastry brush to wipe down the sides of the pan to remove any sugar crystals that may form. If your heat source is uneven, gently rotate the pan occasionally so the sugar heats evenly.

CONTINUED

Pay close attention to the color of the mixture as it starts to caramelize. Once it begins to change color from clear to a light golden hue it will continue to darken quickly, so don't stray from the pot during this critical time. The mixture will continue to darken to a light amber, then deeper still to a rich reddish brown. At that point, immediately remove from the heat and carefully add the reduced pear juice. Because the caramel is very hot, the mixture will bubble and sputter, so you might want to wear oven mitts. Using a long-handled wooden spoon, stir vigorously until the sauce is completely smooth. Set aside to cool slightly.

TO MAKE THE POACHED PEARS: Peel the pears and cut them in half lengthwise. With a melon baller or small spoon, remove the core from each. Put the pears in a bowl, pour the lemon juice over them, and toss gently to coat.

Bring 2 cups of the water to a boil, then let stand until cooled to 160°F. In a heatproof bowl or teapot, combine the tea and water and let steep for 4 minutes.

Immediately strain the tea into a large saucepan. Stir in the sugar and the remaining 1 cup cold water and bring to a simmer over medium heat. Lower the heat and simmer, stirring occasionally, until the sugar has dissolved, about 2 minutes. Add the pears and simmer, gently turning the pears occasionally, until they are easily pierced with a fork, 12 to 15 minutes. Drain the pears, discarding the poaching liquid, and transfer to a bowl to cool.

Spoon 2 pears halves into each of four dishes, then drizzle the sauce over the top before serving.

Chocolate-Tahini Timbales

Überchef Thomas Keller, who popularized these little chocolate morsels, calls them *bouchons*, which is French for "corks." They're less than 2 inches tall, which somehow makes them disappear mysteriously. This variation involves using tahini, a velvety sesame paste, in place of butter. The batter is baked in timbale or baba molds. You'll need to have enough 2- to 3-ounce flexible, nonstick silicone timbale or baba molds to make two dozen timbales at a time.

································{ **MAKES ABOUT 24** }································

4 ounces semisweet baking chocolate, coarsely chopped

½ cup unsweetened plain soymilk

⅔ cup Kahlúa or other coffee liqueur

½ cup tahini

1 teaspoon pure vanilla extract

1½ cups all-purpose flour

1 cup powdered sugar, plus more for dusting

1½ teaspoons baking powder

⅓ cup Dutch-process cocoa powder

½ teaspoon salt

Preheat the oven to 350°F.

Put the chocolate in a medium heatproof bowl. In a small saucepan, heat the soymilk over medium heat until it begins to steam and almost comes to a boil. Pour the soymilk over the chopped chocolate, then add the Kahlúa, tahini, and vanilla. Let stand for 1 minute, then stir until the mixture is smooth and the chocolate is entirely melted.

Sift the flour, powdered sugar, baking powder, cocoa, and salt together into a large bowl. Add the chocolate mixture and stir gently until just combined. Transfer the mixture to a pastry bag without a tip or a resealable plastic bag with one corner snipped off.

CONTINUED

Put about two dozen timbale molds on a baking sheet (the number of molds per pan varies, so just get as close to two dozen as you can). Pipe the batter into the molds, filling each about two-thirds full.

Bake for 15 to 20 minutes, until the tops are firm but the inside is still slightly soft (test by inserting a wooden skewer or toothpick). Transfer the molds to a wire rack and let cool for 5 minutes, then invert the molds and let the timbales cool completely, about 15 minutes. Lift off the molds and dust the timbales with powdered sugar. These treats are best eaten the day they're made.

Piñon Tart

Pine nuts, piñons, or pignolia—no matter what name you call them by, these seeds of certain species of pine have a buttery, subtly resinous flavor and indescribable texture that nicely complements the otherwise sweet, sugary filling of this tart.

{ **MAKES ONE 9-INCH TART; SERVES 6** }

TART SHELL

1¼ **cups all-purpose flour, plus more for dusting**

2 **teaspoons sugar**

½ **teaspoon salt**

½ **cup cold vegan shortening, diced**

2 to 4 **tablespoons ice water**

FILLING

½ **cup sugar**

⅓ **cup agave syrup**

1 **teaspoon salt**

¾ **cup cold vegan shortening, diced**

¾ **cup raw cashew pieces (4 ounces)**

1½ **ounces extra-firm tofu, crumbled**

1 **tablespoon extra-virgin olive oil**

1 **teaspoon fresh lemon juice**

½ **teaspoon baking soda**

1½ **cups pine nuts (6 ounces), toasted (see Tip, page 101)**

TO MAKE THE TART SHELL: In a food processor, combine the flour, sugar, salt, and shortening and pulse until evenly blended. Add the ice water 1 tablespoon at a time while continuing to pulse. Stop just as the dough starts to come together, and don't under any circumstances pulse longer than 30 seconds, as this will adversely affect the texture of the pastry. Test by pinching a bit of dough with your fingers. If it sticks together, it's ready. If not, add more water, 1 tablespoon at a time.

Transfer the dough to a work surface and gently pat it into a disk. Wrap in plastic wrap and refrigerate for at least 1 hour and up to overnight.

Transfer the dough to a lightly floured work surface and roll into an 11-inch round; alternatively, you can sandwich the dough between two sheets of parchment paper for rolling. Lay the dough in a 9-inch tart pan with a removable bottom and gently press it against the bottom and sides of the pan. Trim any overhanging edges by rolling the rolling pin over the top of the pan. Cover with plastic wrap and refrigerate for 15 minutes.

Preheat the oven to 325°F.

MEANWHILE, MAKE THE FILLING:
In a medium saucepan over medium heat, combine the sugar, agave syrup, and salt and cook, whisking constantly, until the sugar dissolves. Add the shortening and whisk until incorporated. Transfer the mixture to a medium bowl and let cool for 30 minutes.

In a food processor, combine the cashews, tofu, olive oil, and lemon juice and process until smooth. Whisk the mixture into the cooled syrup. Add the baking soda and whisk again to combine.

Put the tart pan on a rimmed baking sheet. Scatter the pine nuts over the bottom of the crust, then gently pour the cashew mixture over the pine nuts. Bake for about 1 hour, until the crust is golden brown and the center is set but still slightly loose. If the crust browns too quickly, cover the edges with foil. Transfer the tart to a wire rack and let cool completely before slicing and serving.

CHAPTER 5

Very Late Night

Limoncello

I've been concocting this bright yellow Italian digestif for years. Each holiday season, friends and clients eagerly await their own little bottle of my hand-crafted limoncello. It's traditionally served in small glasses after dinner, ice-cold right out of the freezer. Don't let anyone tell you they are too tired for a quick nip or couldn't possibly consume something more. I guarantee that as soon as they've had a sip or two, the party will start all over again. Resist substituting 80-proof vodka. It won't extract the oils from the lemon rinds in quite the same way.

················{ **MAKES 2 LITERS** }················

Zest from 2 pounds of lemons (yellow part only), preferably organic (see Tip)

1 liter 100-proof vodka

3 cups sugar

3 cups water

Combine the lemon zest and vodka in a large bowl. Cover and let steep for 1 week at room temperature.

In a large saucepan over medium heat, combine the sugar and water and cook, stirring, until the sugar has dissolved. Let cool to room temperature, then add the syrup to the vodka mixture and stir until thoroughly combined. Strain the mixture, discarding the lemon, then decant into two clean 1-liter bottles with tight lids.

Refrigerate for 1 month to allow the flavors to develop, then transfer the limoncello to the freezer so it will be ready to be served ice-cold in a shot or aperitif glass.

TIP: If you use nonorganic lemons, soak them in lukewarm water with lemon juice, vinegar, or an organic citrus-based vegetable cleaning solution for several minutes, then scrub gently and rinse with fresh water.

Shiso Leaf Martini

A sexy drink late at night, or anytime for that matter, can be a great conversation starter. You may already be familiar with shiso, the scallop-edged dark green leaf that makes an appearance in Japanese dishes. Here, the shiso leaf (from the plant also known as *Perilla frutescens*, but that's a turnoff) infuses this vodka martini with a minty, basil-inflected bite that is way more potent than mere sake. *Kanpai!*

{ **SERVES 2** }

8 **ounces vodka**

7 **fresh shiso leaves**

 Ice cubes

1½ **ounces dry vermouth**

½ **ounce fresh lime juice**

 Dash of Angostura bitters (optional)

Combine the vodka and 5 of the shiso leaves in a jar, cover tightly, and infuse for at least 8 hours and up to overnight.

Chill two martini glasses in the freezer for at least 10 minutes.

When ready to serve, discard the steeped shiso leaves. Fill a cocktail shaker with ice, then add the infused vodka, vermouth, lime juice, and bitters (if using). Shake vigorously until well chilled, about 10 seconds. Strain into the chilled glasses and float a shiso leaf in each glass as a garnish.

Hazelnut Halvah

Halvah is made from tahini, sugar, and nuts. I've replaced the traditional pistachios with toasted hazelnuts, which gives it a Pacific Northwest vibe. This sweet, Middle Eastern delicacy can be enjoyed right away, but letting it set in the refrigerator for a couple of days allows a miraculous crystallization to take place. Use a clean, sharp knife to slice the halvah, and enjoy its flaky texture.

MAKES 1 LOAF; SERVES 8 TO 10

1 cup hazelnuts (4 ounces), toasted and skinned (see Tip) and finely chopped

3 cups tahini

1 teaspoon pure vanilla extract

2 cups sugar

1 cup water

Line a 9-by-5-inch loaf pan with plastic wrap or oiled parchment paper, allowing some to hang over on each side of the pan.

In a large bowl, combine the hazelnuts, tahini, and vanilla and stir until well mixed.

In a medium saucepan, combine the sugar and water and cook over medium-high heat, stirring occasionally, until the mixture reaches 240°F on a candy thermometer. Slowly pour the hot sugar syrup into the tahini mixture while stirring constantly, and continue to stir until the mixture is well combined and starts to harden. Immediately transfer the mixture to the prepared pan and smooth the surface with an offset spatula or the back of a spoon.

Let the halvah cool before slicing and serving. Or, better yet, cool, then fold the overhanging wrap over the top of the halvah and refrigerate for at least 2 days before serving. Use a sharp knife to cut enough halvah for each serving, then rewrap the remainder and return it to the refrigerator, where it will keep for up to 3 weeks.

TIP: To toast and skin hazelnuts, spread them in a single layer on a rimmed baking sheet and bake at 350°F for 10 minutes. Transfer to a clean kitchen towel, fold the towel over the nuts, and rub vigorously to remove their skins.

Dates

WITH COFFEE CREMA

I envy people who can drink a double shot of espresso after a late-night meal and still fall asleep when they go to bed. I have never been able to enjoy that ritual without being kept awake for the next twenty-four hours. Depending on how well you and your guests tolerate caffeine, you can make this dessert, an unusual pairing of dates and espresso, with decaf, or enjoy it earlier in the day.

{ **SERVES 6** }

24 Halawi or Medjool dates, pitted

2 cups freshly brewed espresso or strong coffee

20 cardamom pods, lightly crushed

1 teaspoon sugar

COFFEE CREMA

½ cup coconut cream (see Tip)

6 ounces soft silken tofu

1 tablespoon instant espresso powder

1 teaspoon pure vanilla extract

¼ cup sugar

Put the dates in a small heatproof bowl. In a small saucepan, combine the espresso, cardamom pods, and sugar. Bring to a boil over medium-high heat, stirring occasionally. Immediately remove from the heat and allow to steep for 15 minutes. Strain the mixture, discarding the cardamom pods, then pour it over the dates. Let cool, then cover and refrigerate for at least 1 hour and up to overnight.

TO MAKE THE COFFEE CREMA: In a blender or food processor, combine the coconut cream, tofu, espresso powder, vanilla, and sugar and blend until smooth.

Divide the crema among six serving bowls. Arrange 4 dates on top of the crema in each bowl, then drizzle with the remaining liquid from the soaked dates. Serve immediately.

TIP: Most commercial versions of coconut cream are full of nasty additives. For a healthier alternative, simply refrigerate a can of organic coconut milk overnight and skim the cream off the top the next day.

Maple-Chipotle Pecan Popcorn

This ain't no Cracker Jack (so, alas, there's also no prize inside). However, this grown-up caramel corn is so addictive that I've written the recipe to yield a substantial amount. It's got a bit of a chile bite to it, so please adjust according to your heat tolerance.

{ **MAKES 10 CUPS; SERVES 4** }

- **4 tablespoons canola oil**
- **⅓ cup popcorn kernels**
- **1 cup raw pecans (4 ounces)**
- **1 dried chipotle mora chile, or to taste, or ½ teaspoon ground chiles**
- **6 tablespoons vegan shortening**
- **1½ cups maple syrup**
- **½ teaspoon salt**

Preheat the oven to 350°F. Line a rimmed baking sheet with foil, then lightly coat the foil and a wooden spoon with 1 tablespoon of the canola oil.

In a large saucepan with a lid, heat the remaining 3 tablespoons oil over medium-high heat. Add the popcorn kernels, cover, and cook, shaking the pan occasionally to prevent burning. When the popping slows to 3 to 5 seconds between pops, remove from the heat and let cool for 1 to 2 minutes. Transfer the popcorn to a large bowl, removing any unpopped kernels.

Spread the pecans in a single layer on a rimmed baking sheet. Bake for 7 to 8 minutes, until lightly toasted and fragrant. When cool enough to handle, coarsely chop the pecans. Add them to the popcorn and toss to combine.

Meanwhile, use a spice mill to finely grind the chile. In a small, heavy saucepan, melt the shortening over medium heat. Stir in the maple syrup, ground chile, and salt, then bring to a boil and cook, without stirring, until the mixture reaches 300°F on a candy thermometer, 15 to 20 minutes.

Pour the syrup over the popcorn and quickly stir with the oiled spoon to evenly coat. Immediately spread the mixture on the prepared pan. Let cool completely, then break into bite-size pieces. Store in an airtight container at room temperature for up to 3 days.

Chocolate Truffles

Although truffles are romantic and indulgent, they're also relatively easy to make. Here are three decadent variations on the theme: espresso-cocoa, raspberry-almond, and chile–pine nut. Once you've made these, experiment with your own flavor combinations and use them to seduce someone special.

··{ **MAKES 36** }··

2 pounds bittersweet chocolate (at least 65% cacao), coarsely chopped

½ cup vegan shortening

¼ teaspoon salt

2½ cups unsweetened plain soymilk

2 teaspoons instant espresso powder

3 teaspoons water

1 tablespoon Chambord or other raspberry liqueur

1 teaspoon New Mexico chile powder

½ cup Dutch-process cocoa powder

½ cup almonds (2 ounces), toasted (see Tip, page 101) and chopped

½ cup pine nuts (2 ounces), toasted (see Tip, page 101) and finely chopped

In a large heatproof bowl, combine the chocolate, shortening, and salt. In a small saucepan, heat the soymilk over medium heat until it begins to emit steam and almost comes to a boil, then pour it over the chocolate mixture. Let stand for 5 minutes, then whisk until the mixture is smooth and the chocolate is entirely melted.

Evenly divide the chocolate mixture into three small bowls. Dissolve the espresso powder in 2 teaspoons of the water, then stir the mixture into the first bowl until evenly incorporated. Stir the Chambord into the second bowl until evenly incorporated. Stir the chile powder into the remaining 1 teaspoon water and stir the mixture into the third bowl until evenly incorporated. Cover the bowls and refrigerate until cooled, 3 to 4 hours.

CONTINUED

Line a baking sheet with parchment paper. Using a melon baller or small scoop, drop tablespoons of each chocolate mixture onto the sheet, keeping the three flavors separate (you may want to use three separate baking sheets or plates). Refrigerate until set, about 1 hour.

Put the cocoa powder, almonds, and pine nuts in three small separate bowls. Quickly roll the mounds of chocolate into balls, still keeping the flavors separated. They should end up being roughly 1½ inches in diameter. Roll the espresso truffles in the cocoa powder to evenly coat, the raspberry truffles in the chopped almonds to evenly coat, and the chile truffles in the pine nuts to evenly coat. If not serving the truffles right away, store them in an airtight container in the refrigerator, where they will keep for up to 1 week. Bring the truffles to room temperature before serving.

Chocolate Sea Salt Tart

What can I say about the taste of salty-sweet? Maybe it's the sixth taste after sweet, sour, salty, bitter, and umami (the latter sometimes characterized as savory). The Maldon sea salt that graces the top of this chocolaty tart is like jewels on a crown. Harvested in Maldon, England, these pure, white salt crystals look like snowflakes that have fallen on your sweetly sophisticated dessert.

{ **MAKES ONE 9-INCH TART; SERVES 6 TO 8** }

COCOA TART SHELL

- 1½ **cups all-purpose flour**
- ½ **cup powdered sugar**
- 2 **tablespoons natural cocoa powder**
- ¼ **teaspoon salt**
- ½ **cup cold vegan shortening, diced**
- 1 to 3 **tablespoons ice water or more as needed**

FILLING

- 1¼ **pounds dark chocolate, coarsely chopped**
- 2½ **cups unsweetened plain soymilk**
- 1 **tablespoon instant espresso powder**
- 1 **teaspoon salt**

   Maldon sea salt or any high-quality flake sea salt for garnish

Preheat the oven to 350°F.

TO MAKE THE TART SHELL: In a food processor, combine the flour, powdered sugar, cocoa powder, salt, and shortening and pulse until the mixture is evenly blended. Add the water 1 tablespoon at a time while continuing to pulse. Stop as soon as the dough starts to come together. Test by pinching a bit of the dough with your fingers. If it sticks together, it's ready. If not, add more water. Alternatively, you can mix the dough by hand. Combine the flour, powdered sugar, cocoa powder, and salt in a large bowl. Add the shortening and use a fork or a pastry blender to incorporate until crumbly. Add the water 1 tablespoon at a time and continue mixing until the dough comes together, adding more water as needed and using the same pinch test as described.

CONTINUED

Transfer the dough directly into a 9-inch tart pan and gently press it into the pan. Begin by building up the sides to form a ¼-inch-thick wall of dough. Then distribute the remaining dough evenly over the bottom of the pan. Wrap a 1-cup measuring cup with plastic wrap and use the bottom to evenly press the dough into the bottom of the pan. Prick the bottom of the tart shell with the tines of a fork 12 to 15 times to prevent the crust from puffing up during baking. Cover with plastic wrap and refrigerate for 15 minutes.

Line the tart shell with parchment paper and spread pie weights or dried beans over the paper, pushing the bulk of the weights to the edges of the shell. Bake for 20 minutes. Remove the weights and bake for 4 to 5 minutes, until the bottom of the shell is firm and dry. Remove from the oven and let rest while you prepare the filling.

TO MAKE THE FILLING: Put the chocolate in a medium heatproof bowl. In a small saucepan, heat the soymilk over medium heat until it begins to steam and almost comes to a boil. Add the espresso powder and salt and stir until dissolved. Pour the soymilk over the chocolate and let stand for 1 minute, then stir until the mixture is smooth and the chocolate is entirely melted.

Pour the filling into the baked tart shell and use an offset spatula to spread it evenly. Give the tart a gentle but firm rap on the counter to settle the filling and remove any air bubbles. Let the tart cool to room temperature, which should take about 30 minutes. When it's completely cool, sprinkle the sea salt evenly over the top and serve.

Charoset Tart

When I was a child, Passover seders seemed to go on forever. This ceremonial meal tells the story of the exodus from ancient Egypt by the Israelites and uses special foods as part of the narrative (and to keep guests from passing out at the table). One of my favorites among these foods has always been charoset, a thick paste of fruit, wine, and nuts that symbolizes the mortar enslaved Hebrews used when building the pyramids for the pharaoh. Taken off the Seder plate, and made into a tart, this Sephardic version of charoset, with dates and figs, thankfully does not resemble mortar. And no matter how you were raised, this charoset tart is delicious anytime of year.

MAKES ONE 9-INCH TART; SERVES 6 TO 8

1 unbaked Tart Shell (page 194)

FRANGIPANE

1 cup raw almonds (4½ ounces)

½ cup vegan shortening

½ cup sugar

3 tablespoons Cognac

1 teaspoon pure vanilla extract

1 tablespoon all-purpose flour

1½ ounces soft silken tofu

½ teaspoon baking powder

FILLING

6 dried black Mission figs, stemmed and coarsely chopped

6 dates, pitted and coarsely chopped

6 dried apricots, coarsely chopped

1 tablespoon grated orange zest

2 Granny Smith apples, peeled and diced

⅓ cup raw almonds (1½ ounces), coarsely chopped

½ cup raw walnuts (2 ounces), coarsely chopped

1 teaspoon grated peeled fresh ginger

½ teaspoon ground cinnamon

1 tablespoon agave syrup

1 tablespoon fresh lemon juice

5 tablespoons red wine or Cognac

3 tablespoons apricot jam

Preheat the oven to 400°F.

TO MAKE THE FRANGIPANE: In a food processor, pulse the almonds until finely ground. Add the shortening, sugar, Cognac, vanilla, flour, tofu, and baking powder and process until smooth.

Spread the frangipane evenly over the bottom of the chilled tart shell, then put the tart shell in the refrigerator while you prepare the filling.

TO MAKE THE FILLING: In a food processor (no need to clean it out), combine the figs, dates, apricots, orange zest, apples, almonds, walnuts, ginger, cinnamon, agave syrup, lemon juice, and wine and pulse until coarsely chopped but not transformed into a paste.

Spread the filling evenly over the frangipane. Put the tart pan on a rimmed baking sheet or cover the bottom with foil and bake for 45 minutes, until firm. If the edges of the crust brown too quickly, cover them with foil. Put the tart on a wire rack to cool.

A few minutes before the end of the baking time, heat the apricot jam in a small saucepan over medium heat until it melts into a syrup, 2 to 3 minutes. Brush the apricot jam over the warm tart as a glaze, then let the tart cool before slicing and serving.

Resources

No matter where you live, the Internet can be your cybersourcing friend. Considering the seemingly unlimited options available online, this list is just a jumping-off point for the harder-to-find items included in the recipes. Note that I've divvied things up into edibles (food ingredients) and equipment. And for those of you who were inspired by the Food Sourcing Pyramid (see Ingredient Sourcing, page 15), I've included a few resources that will help get you started on finding alternative food sources. Happy shopping!

EDIBLES

ANSON MILLS

ansonmills.com
Milled organic heirloom grains, including flours, semolina, and polenta.

BOB'S RED MILL

bobsredmill.com
A wide variety of grains, beans, and other dried goods, including vital wheat gluten, nutritional yeast, tapioca starch, garbanzo bean flour, polenta, and semolina flour.

CHADO TEA ROOM

chadotea.com
Matcha, Lapsang souchong, Darjeeling, Earl Grey, jasmine, and many other teas.

CHOCOVIVO

chocovivo.com
Organic chocolate.

CLARO'S ITALIAN MARKET

claros.com
Imported and domestic Italian specialty foods, including San Marzano tomatoes, Arborio rice, and pine nuts.

EARTH BALANCE

earthbalancenatural.com
Vegan margarine and shortening.

EDEN

edenfoods.com
Matcha, mirin, soymilk, agar flakes, and canned butter beans, garbanzo beans, and kidney beans.

FOOD DEPOT

efooddepot.com
A wide variety of international ingredients, including rose water, orange blossom water, pomegranate molasses, saffron, sumac, tahini, basmati rice, cardamom, grape leaves in brine, and coconut milk.

GREENBAR COLLECTIVE

greenbar.biz
Organic liquors, including vodka, tequila, and liqueurs.

HOME BREW HEAVEN

homebrewheaven.com

Champagne yeast.

IGOURMET

igourmet.com

A wide variety of gourmet foods, including hazelnut oil, organic dried fruits, and pine nuts.

IHERB

iherb.com

A wide variety of natural products, including agar flakes and powder, nutritional yeast, agave syrup, and lecithin.

KING ARTHUR FLOUR

kingarthurflour.com

Specialty baking goods, including instant espresso powder, bread flour, yeast, and baking equipment.

K&L WINE MERCHANTS

klwines.com

Wines and spirits, including aquavit, Angostura bitters, and crème de cassis.

LA VIGNE FRUITS

lavignefruits.com

Blood orange juice and fresh oranges.

MATCHA SOURCE

matchasource.com

Matcha.

MELISSA'S PRODUCE

melissas.com

A variety of fresh and dried fruits and vegetables, including blood oranges, crystallized ginger, dried chiles (chipotle, de árbol, guajillo, pasilla, and others), Jerusalem artichokes, pomegranates, serrano chiles, shiso leaves, and tomatillos, as well as nuts, herbs and spices, tofu, lemon verbena, and Latin American products.

MEXGROCER

mexgrocer.com

Authentic and hard-to-find Mexican products, including Ibarra chocolate.

MIDWEST HOMEBREWING AND WINEMAKING SUPPLIES

midwestsupplies.com

Champagne yeast.

MY SPICE SAGE

myspicesage.com

A wide selection of spices, herbs, seasonings, and other ingredients, including smoked Spanish paprika, lavender, and dried chiles.

THE OLIVE OIL SOURCE

oliveoilsource.com

Organic olive oil from California, as well as vinegars.

PACIFIC RIM GOURMET

pacificrimgourmet.com

Exotic ingredients from the Pacific Rim, including Vietnamese rice paper spring roll wrappers and coconut milk.

SALTWORKS

saltworks.us

A wide variety of gourmet salts, including Maldon sea salt.

THE SPICE HOUSE

thespicehouse.com

High-quality herbs and spices, including sumac, Aleppo pepper, saffron, and lavender.

SPICE STATION

spicestationsilverlake.com

Herbs, spices, seasonings, and teas, including Darjeeling tea, sumac, and lavender.

WORLD SPICE MERCHANTS

worldspice.com

Herbs, spices, and teas, including sumac, dried chiles, lavender, and Lapsang souchong, Darjeeling, and jasmine teas.

EQUIPMENT

THE BOSTON SHAKER

thebostonshaker.com

Cocktail shakers, strainers, glasses, and measuring jiggers.

CHAMPION JUICER

championjuicer.com

Masticating juicer.

CRATE AND BARREL

crateandbarrel.com

Cookware, bakeware, small appliances, cutlery, storage containers, gadgets, and utensils.

CUISINART

cuisinartwebstore.com

Food processors, cookware, blenders, stand mixers, and ice-cream makers.

CULINARY DISTRICT

culinarydistrict.com

Cookware, bakeware, small appliances, cutlery, storage containers, gadgets, and utensils.

HOME BREW HEAVEN

homebrewheaven.com

Flip-top bottles.

HUROM

slowjuicer.com

Slow Juicer juice extractor.

KEREKES

bakedeco.com

Flexible silicone baba pans for timbales.

MIDWEST HOMEBREWING AND WINEMAKING SUPPLIES

midwestsupplies.com

Flip-top bottles.

THE OLIVE OIL SOURCE

Oliveoilsource.com

Bottles and spouts.

OMEGA

omegajuicers.com

A variety of juicers.

SUR LA TABLE

surlatable.com

Cookware, bakeware, small appliances, cutlery, storage containers, gadgets, and utensils.

WILLIAMS-SONOMA

williams-sonoma.com

Bouchon molds, cookware, bakeware, small appliances, cutlery, storage containers, gadgets, and utensils.

ALTERNATIVE FOOD SOURCING RESOURCES

HILLSIDE PRODUCE COOPERATIVE

hillsideproducecooperative.org/a-chapter-near-you

A guide to starting a cooperative produce exchange in your own neighborhood.

HYPERLOCAVORE

hyperlocavore.com

Yard-sharing matchmaker site connecting people interested in sharing surplus produce, garden space, yard skills, and resources.

LOCAL HARVEST

localharvest.org

An online resource for finding locally grown produce. Search nationwide for farms, CSAs (community-supported agriculture sites), farmers' markets, and grocery stores and food co-ops that may carry local produce.

SHARED EARTH

sharedearth.com

An organization that connects landowners with gardeners and farmers.

UNITED STATES DEPARTMENT OF AGRICULTURE, AGRICULTURAL MARKETING SERVICE

apps.ams.usda.gov/FarmersMarkets

A national, searchable database of farmers' markets.

Index

Table of Equivalents

The exact equivalents in the following tables have been rounded for convenience.

LIQUID/DRY MEASUREMENTS

U.S.	METRIC
¼ teaspoon	1.25 milliliters
½ teaspoon	2.5 milliliters
1 teaspoon	5 milliliters
1 tablespoon (3 teaspoons)	15 milliliters
1 fluid ounce (2 tablespoons)	30 milliliters
¼ cup	60 milliliters
⅓ cup	80 milliliters
½ cup	120 milliliters
1 cup	240 milliliters
1 pint (2 cups)	480 milliliters
1 quart (4 cups, 32 ounces)	960 milliliters
1 gallon (4 quarts)	3.84 liters
1 ounce (by weight)	28 grams
1 pound	448 grams
2.2 pounds	1 kilogram

LENGTHS

U.S.	METRIC
⅛ inch	3 millimeters
¼ inch	6 millimeters
½ inch	12 millimeters
1 inch	2.5 centimeters

OVEN TEMPERATURE

FAHRENHEIT	CELSIUS	GAS
250	120	½
275	140	1
300	150	2
325	160	3
350	180	4
375	190	5
400	200	6
425	220	7
450	230	8
475	240	9
500	260	10